THE BEST IN TENT CAMPING

A GUIDE FOR CAR CAMPERS WHO HATE RVs, CONCRETE SLABS, AND LOUD PORTABLE STEREOS

WASHINGTON

JEANNE LOUISE PYLE

MENASHA RIDGE PRESS
BIRMINGHAM, ALABAMA

Printed in the United States of America
Published by Menasha Ridge Press
Distributed by the Globe Pequot Press
First edition, first printing

Library of Congress Cataloging-in-Publication Data is
available from the Library of Congress.

ISBN 0-89732-569-9

Cover and text design by Ian Szymkowiak, Palace Press International, Inc.
Cover photo by Monserrate J. Schwartz/Alamy
Maps by Jennie Zehmer

Menasha Ridge Press
P.O. Box 43673
Birmingham, Alabama 35243
www.menasharidge.com

THE BEST IN TENT CAMPING

WASHINGTON

Other titles in the series:

TABLE OF CONTENTS

OLYMPIC PENINSULA AND SOUTHWESTERN WASHINGTON

PUGET SOUND

NORTHERN CASCADES AND ENVIRONS

CENTRAL CASCADES AND ENVIRONS

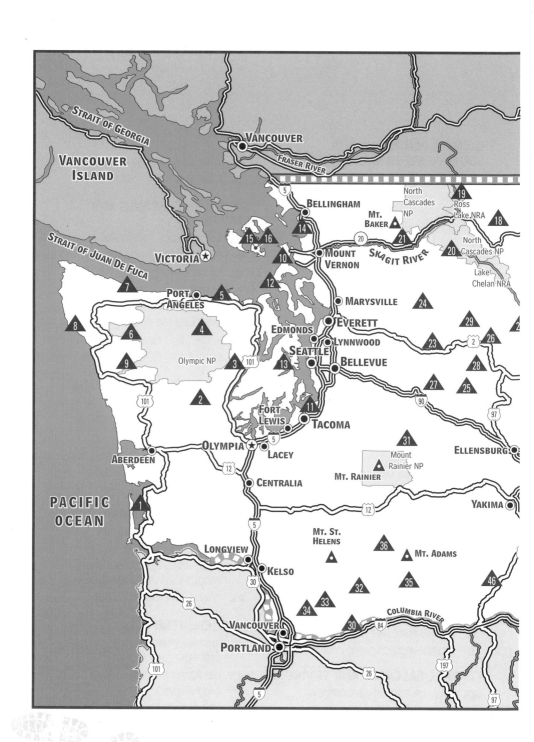

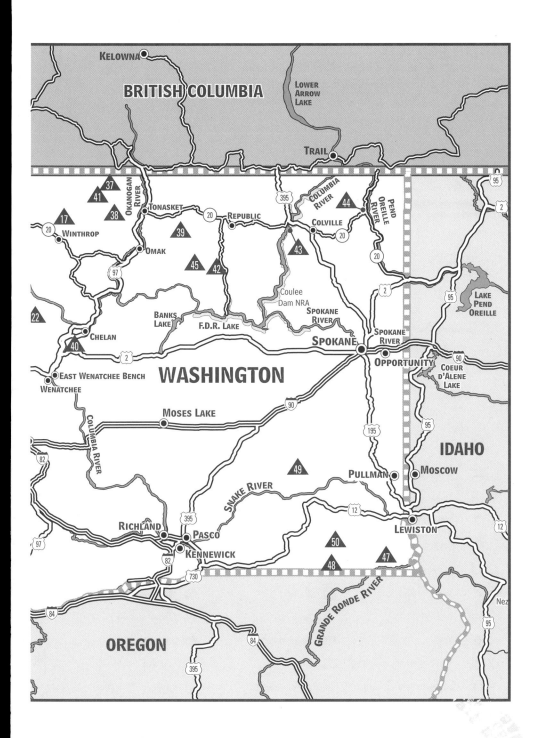

MAP LEGEND

WHITE WOLF	Individual tent and RV campsites within campground area	Table Rock	NATIONAL FOREST	STATE PARK
Campground name and location		Other nearby campgrounds	Public lands	

Interstate highways	US highways	State roads	County roads	Service roads	Other roads	Unpaved or gravel roads
64	19 219	325	219	SR-219	MAIN ST.	

Boardwalk	Political boundary	Railroads	Hiking, biking, or horse trail	Swift Creek
				River or stream

Asheville	N	Ward Lake
City or town	Indicates North	Ocean, lake, or bay

Bridge or tunnel	Playground	Picnic area
Amphitheater	Parking	Sheltered picnic area
Falls or rapids	Marina or boat ramp	Spring/well
Food	Fire ring	Dishwater disposal
Restroom	Telephone	Summit or lookout
Water access	Laundry	Bathhouse
Gate	Cemetery	Dump station
Trash	Swimming	No swimming
Wheelchair accessible	Horse trail	Stables
Hospital/medical care	Postal dropoff	Ranger office

ACKNOWLEDGMENTS

I **AM GRATEFUL** to all who provided me with varying amounts of information, insights, suggestions, warnings, guidance, and encouragement to bring this book and its companion, *The Best in Tent Camping: Oregon*, to fruition.

Without the assistance of the National Forest Service, National Park Service, Washington State Parks, Department of Natural Resources, and various other agency staff, I would have floundered endlessly where they nimbly and knowledgeably answered my needs.

To Joan Fish, a veteran outdoorswoman and native Washingtonian with an ever-ready enthusiasm for yet another "Jeanne-and-Joan adventure"—and a blessedly flexible schedule.

To Bill Fry, who, I think, actually enjoyed getting "outside of his box" on a few occasions.

To my stalwart Volvo station wagon, serving without a single complaint and under the utmost duress. Truly a wonder of a car!

WHEN *The Best in Tent Camping: Oregon* was published in the spring of 2004, I was asked by an interviewer on a Portland radio station why it is that, in this modern, sophisticated, technologically advanced world, so many of us are still drawn to the pleasures of getting out into the woods and sitting around a campfire.

I answered, "I hope because of its simplicity." That was probably too simple of an answer, but we only had three minutes of airtime, it was an unrehearsed interview, and how deep can you go on the spot? It got me pondering, however. Maybe in our subconscious, it's our way of doing penance for what we haven't left so simple elsewhere. Maybe we're paying guilty homage to those vestiges of a land that was once unspoiled. Maybe it's the innate pioneer call of the last frontier. Maybe we go . . . because it's there.

Whatever your reason for seeking the great outdoors, do me a favor. Keep it simple. Keep it clean. And, most important to me, keep it quiet. Enjoying the natural state of things includes the natural sounds. Listen to them, appreciate them, respect them, and teach your kids to do the same. Enough said. OK, one more thing: slow down!! Those 15- and 25-mph signs are actually there for a good reason, even if you don't mind beating your brand-new SUV to pieces. There. No more sermonizing. I did that (quite unapologetically, thank you) in the Oregon book, as those of you who have already picked up that copy know.

For now, I hope you take every oppotunity to enjoy this newly updated and expanded edition of Oregon's companion, *The Best in Tent Camping: Washington*, which was, unfortunately, delayed a year. Forest fires and floods in the summer and fall of 2003 knocked a number of my planned entries out of commission, and I was unable to get back out to investigate until the spring and summer of 2004. In some places, the damage was pure tragedy, in others repair is under way, and in still others, the facilities may have survived but the ambience was highly compromised.

As a result, I scrambled a bit to find acceptable alternatives and still meet my deadline—roll of publisher's eyes—and I hope you'll agree that I came out smelling more like a pine forest than a dirty pair of hiking socks! So far, the natural disasters failed to make mincemeat of my very best attempts to bring you the most current news from the camping scene, and I refuse to be held personally responsible for what effect Mount St. Helens might have on the state of things. If she's busted her gut again by the time you've bought your copy, all bets are off. Look at the bright side: you'll have an instant collector's item on your hands! And I have built-in job security. . . .

As with the Oregon edition, many of the original entries in the combined edition, *The Best in Tent Camping: Washington and Oregon,* are stalwart survivors of the minimum criteria and the subjective rating system. Each has been updated as best as possible with any fresh information provided by the respective managing agencies. The new entries were researched either in the summer and fall of 2003 or in the spring and summer of 2004 and provide an eclectic range of camping options: from sites in the busier state parks—with easy access yet beautiful settings—to those in the remote sanctity of Little Pend Oreille National Wildlife Refuge.

Enjoy them while you can. The next four years may do more damage than a spewing volcano!

Happy camping,

—Jeanne Louise Pyle
November, 2004

A Word about This Book and
Washington Tent Camping

INTRODUCTION

From wide sandy beaches to volatile, snow-capped volcanoes to narrow river gorges, Washington rivals its neighbor Oregon (see *The Best in Tent Camping: Oregon*) as a place of different but equally unparalleled natural beauty and diversity. As with Oregon, extremes of climate, terrain, and vegetation can often be experienced in just a single day's outing. The campgrounds included in this book are representative of the variety that makes Washington a beloved destination for those who seek outstanding outdoor adventures—either for a quick weekend getaway or an extended tour.

And for those who seek that adventure farther afield than most and who value an experience that is long on solitude, serenity, and space, be aware that you may have to drive farther and climb higher and plan more creatively. Although Washington ranks second nationally behind Alaska in designated wilderness acreage, it still constitutes only a little more than 10 percent of the state's total land. With more and more people flocking to the scenic natural splendors beyond city limits, this pushes the capacity for a true wilderness experience to new boundaries.

Encountering RVs in the most unlikely of places as I did in my travels to research this book in 2003 and 2004, one has to wonder if it isn't more comforting to think of wilderness as a state of mind rather than an actual place. I have observed that for some tent campers, it is satisfaction enough just to pitch a tent alongside several hundred others in midsummer at the busy nearby state park. For others, simply being able to drive to the campground immediately eliminates it from consideration. If your sentiment lies somewhere between these two extremes, you should find the offerings in this book appealing.

A trend I have noticed in the past few years is a bit of a "good news, bad news" report, but I prefer to look at it as an encouraging sign. In the larger, more developed campgrounds run by the various agencies that have a hand in developing, managing, and maintaining the public lands of Washington, it is now not uncommon to find a loop of sites designated as "tent camping" and another defined as "RV/Trailers." The tent-camping sites are more rustic, without electric hookups, and usually with better vegetation between sites. The bad news is that they often get taken by the overflow of rigs and trailers that get there before the tent campers (certainly not because they're faster) and squeeze themselves into the parking space. One problem solved; another one created. Still, it's good to see that there is sensitivity to two very different styles of camping within the same compound.

Naturally, there are factors besides crowds that affect every camping trip, from a last-minute urge to slip out of town to a backcountry expedition planned months in advance. Here is some information that will prove useful whether you are a first-time camper in Washington or a veteran who can always use a few reminders.

WEST VERSUS EAST

For a traveler new to the state, the most distinctive feature in Washington is the difference in climate, terrain, and to some degree, lifestyle between the western and eastern regions of the state. While this book groups the campgrounds in fairly broad geographical regions simply for locator purposes, west and east here are, by and large, defined by the Pacific Crest National Scenic Trail (PCT), which you'll find on most of the topo and Forest Service maps you will use to explore the areas close to the campground entries. The PCT begins on the United States–Canada border and follows the spine of the Cascade Range down through Washington and Oregon, continuing on into California to its end at the Mexican border. In Washington, it starts on the western edge of the Pasayten Wilderness and plunges due south into fearsome terrain that can make even the most intrepid mountain goat question the sanity of its lifestyle. It exits the state into Oregon a tad more sedately just a few miles east of Beacon Rock State Park (see entry, page 100), crossing the Columbia River over the Bridge of the Gods.

WEATHER

Prevailing conditions year-round in western Washington (with one exception) are mild and damp. Not so much rain, actually, as a healthy supply of gray clouds and mist. The exception is a phenomenon known as the "banana belt," which cuts a swath of drier weather from Sequim on the Olympic Peninsula across the Strait of Juan de Fuca, into the San Juan Islands, catching the western edge of Whidbey Island and Anacortes, continuing northeast over parts of Whatcom County. Late summer and early fall are the most dependable for a lovely string of dry, sunny, warm days just about anywhere in western Washington.

In eastern Washington, conditions are prairie-like at lower elevations, and in the summer, the heat is *on*—searingly hot and dustbowl dry. You'll want to head for the hills, which won't be all that noticeably cooler by day but can get chilly at night. Severe thunderstorms can be the biggest threat to outdoor activity, and this, in turn, can spark instantaneous wildfires and flash floods. At higher elevations on both western and eastern mountain slopes, snow is not uncommon even in midsummer. Sudden changes in weather conditions are always a consideration, so pack for the weather and whatever activities you may be planning.

ROAD CONDITIONS

Many of the campgrounds in this book are reached by minimally maintained access roads. Since we were looking for spots that are somewhat off the beaten path (and away from the routes those dreaded RVs travel), access roads can be rougher than you might expect. Check current road conditions before venturing too far if you are unsure of what you may encounter. And be sure that you have a good current road atlas or Forest Service map with you. The maps in this book are designed to help orient you, nothing more. Although we've provided directions at the end of each entry, you'll find it helpful to have more detailed maps with you when traveling in the territory around most of these campgrounds. Local and district offices that oversee the management of most of these campgrounds are the best source for detailed maps (see Appendix B for more information on these agencies).

RESTRICTIONS

More people using an area usually means more restrictions. State and federal agencies manage most of the campgrounds in this book. Check with the proper authorities for current regulations on recreational activities such as permits for day-use parking, backcountry travel, licenses for hunting and fishing, mountain bikes in designated areas, and so on We have included some restrictions in the Key Information sections of each campground description, but because restrictions can change, you still need to check before you go. Be aware that many National Forest and State Park parking areas now require day-use fees or annual passes. Passes can be purchased at any forest service office, ranger station, park office, and at numerous campgrounds and oudoor retailer outlets.

FIRES

Campfire regulations are subject to seasonal conditions. Usually there are signs posted at campgrounds or ranger district offices. Please be sure you are aware of the current situation, and *never* make a campfire anywhere other than in existing fire pits at developed sites. *Never, ever* toss a match or cigarette idly in the brush or alongside the road. It's not only a littering consideration: A single match can be the destruction of that beautiful forest you were just admiring.

WATER

Many of the campgrounds in this book are remote enough that piped water is not available. No matter how remote you may think you are, don't risk drinking straight from mountain streams, creeks, and lakes. Washington strives to keep its natural waters pure, but they are not immune to that nasty parasite called *Giardia lamblia,* which causes horrific stomach cramps and long-term diarrhea. If you don't have drinking water or purification tablets with you, boil any untreated water for at least five minutes. This will seem like a hassle if you're dry as a bone at the end of a long day of activity, but believe me, it's worth the few minutes of waiting for the agony you will avoid.

THE RATING SYSTEM

Within the scope of the original campground criteria for this book—accessible by car and preferably not by RV, scenic, and as close to a wilderness setting as possible—each campground has its own characteristics. The best way to deal with these varying attributes was to devise a rating system that highlights each campground's best features. On our five-star ranking system, five is the highest rating and one is the lowest. So if you're looking for a campground that is beautiful and achingly quiet, look for five stars in both of those categories. If you're more interested in a campground that has excellent security and cavernous campsites, look for five stars in the spaciousness and security categories. Keep in mind that these ratings are based somewhat on the subjective views of the author and her sources.

BEAUTY

If this category needs any explanation, it is simply to say that the true beauty of a campground is not always what you can see but what you can't see. Or hear. Like a freeway. Or roaring motorboats. Or the *crack, pop, pop, boom* of a rifle range. An equally important factor for me on the beauty scale is the condition of the campground itself and to what extent it has been left in its natural state. Beauty also, of course, takes into consideration any fabulous views of mountains, water, or other natural phenomena.

PRIVACY

No one who enjoys the simplicity of tent camping wants to be walled in on all sides by RVs the size of tractor trailers. This category goes hand in hand with the previous one because part of the beauty of a campsite has to do with the privacy of its surroundings. If you've ever crawled out of your tent to embrace a stunning summer morning in your skivvies and found several pairs of very curious eyes staring at you from the neighbor's picture window, you know what I mean. I look for campsites that are graciously spaced with lots of heavy foliage in between. You usually have to drive a little deeper into the campground complex for these.

SPACIOUSNESS

This is the category you toss the coin on and keep your fingers crossed. I'm not as much of a stickler for this category because I'm happy if there's room to park the car off the main campground road, enough space to pitch a two- or four-person tent in a reasonably flat and dry spot, a picnic table for meal preparation, and a fire pit safely away from the tenting area. At most campgrounds, site spaciousness is sacrificed for site privacy and vice versa. Sometimes you get extremely lucky and have both. Don't be greedy.

QUIET

Again, this category goes along with the beauty of a place. When I go camping, I want to hear the sounds of nature. You know, birds chirping, the wind sighing, a surf crashing, a brook babbling. Call me crazy. . . . It's not always possible to control the noise volume of your fellow campers, so the closer you can get to natural sounds that can drown them out, the better. Actually, when you have a chance to listen to the quiet of nature, you'll find that it is really rather noisy. But what a lovely cacophony!

SECURITY

Quite a few of the campgrounds in this book are in remote and primitive places without on-site security patrol. In essence, you're on your own. Common sense is a great asset in these cases. Don't leave expensive outdoor gear or valuable camera equipment lying around your campsite or even within view inside your car. If you are at a hosted site, you may feel more comfortable leaving any valuables with the host (if they're willing). Or let them know you'll be gone for an extended period so they can keep an eye on your things. Unfortunately, even in lightly camped areas, vandalism is a common camping problem. In many places, the wild animals can do as much damage as a human being. If you leave food inside your tent or around the campsite, don't be surprised if things look slightly ransacked when you return. The most frequent visitors to food-strewn campsites are birds, squirrels, chipmunks, deer, and bears.

CLEANLINESS

By and large, all the campgrounds in this book should rank five stars for this category. Park and Forest Service personnel work hard to keep our campgrounds clean and free of litter and unnecessary debris. The only time they tend to fall a bit short of expectation is on busy summer weekends. This is usually only in the larger, more developed compounds. In more remote areas, the level of cleanliness is most often dependent on the good habits of the campers themselves. Keep that in mind wherever you camp. If the sign says, "Pack it in, pack it out," do as you're told. You can dump your garbage at the first gas fill-up spot. *Don't* expect someone to pick up after you at the campsite.

CHANGES

As with any guidebook, changes in the information provided in these listings are inevitable. It's a good idea to call ahead for the most updated report on the campground you've selected. We would appreciate knowing about any noteworthy changes that you may come across.

OLYMPIC PENINSULA AND SOUTHWESTERN WASHINGTON

BRUCEPORT COUNTY PARK CAMPGROUND

I **HAD JUST ABOUT** given up hope of finding an adequate replacement on the Long Beach Peninsula for Evergreen Court (my entry in the combined edition). This is an area of Washington State so unique in history, landscapes, economic activities, and environmental sensitivity that I felt shortchanged for not being able to have it represented from a tent-camping standpoint.

I had given myself several days to explore this far southwestern region, having ruled out Evergreen Court as no longer meeting my criteria. I kept trying to give Cape Disappointment (formerly Fort Canby State Park) the benefit of the doubt, but it was just too much of a three-ring circus for me. Other options were eliminated either for location, amenities, or for not fitting a tent-camping profile (that is, for being far too RV-oriented). Unfortunately, that is the recreation demographic to which much of this southwestern portion of the state caters.

Discouraged, I was retracing my route north from Long Beach on US 101, following the shoreline of Willapa Bay toward South Bend and Raymond when I spied a sign, "Bruceport County Park," not far past the turnoff to Bay Center.

Hmm, I thought. Never heard of this one before. Hard left into the entrance, and *voilà*!

Allow me to introduce Bruceport County Park. Who knew? Far from metropolitan centers, not listed specifically as a camping park on any maps or in any guidebooks, difficult to track down through Internet sources, easily overlooked if you have your mind set on Long Beach as your destination. I regret that I may be bringing it kicking and screaming into the limelight, but a girl's gotta do what a girl's gotta do. And when you find a hidden gem—that's not really hidden at all, just a little once removed and overshadowed by the

> *Here's an oasis in an otherwise tent camping–parched region with views of Willapa Bay from your bluff-top campsite.*

RATINGS

Beauty: ✿ ✿ ✿ ✿ ✿
Privacy: ✿ ✿ ✿ ✿
Spaciousness: ✿ ✿ ✿ ✿
Quiet: ✿ ✿ ✿ ✿
Security: ✿ ✿ ✿ ✿ ✿
Cleanliness: ✿ ✿ ✿ ✿ ✿

overcommercialized lure of Long Beach—to my mind the find is as much fun as the camping experience itself.

The campground sits on 42 wooded acres of high-bank frontage along Willapa Bay and is a mix of individual tent sites, a stretch of hookup spaces (happily together away from most of the individual sites and guarding the quarter-mile trail to the beach), several group areas (including one that is covered with a barbecue and woodstove reservable in advance), and a grassy primitive area for hikers (not sure how they would get here without a car), cyclists, and motor bikers. The drive in is far enough off US 101 that road noise is not a concern as far as I could hear—always something to consider when camping beside a main thoroughfare.

The best sites are rather obvious—anything from A7 to G2 that line the bank and look out over the wide, estuarine beauty of Willapa Bay. Sites A7 through A12 are more generously spaced. When you get back into the B section, they get tighter, but there is still plenty of vegetation between them, so it feels they are not intruding on each other. You'll be backed up to a gorgeous view, anyway, and everyone else will be similarly distracted. Familiarity breeds camaraderie.

Bruceport is owned by Pacific County Public Works Department and operated by an independent contractor who, along with his mother and sister, handles everything from collecting fees and cleaning the bathrooms to throwing out rowdy campers. Pacific County makes the rules and sets the fees. Mom (Melaine) Mero and her offspring make sure the camping experience brings people back. Their only compensation comes through the camping fees—so right there is a good reason to keep this place busy.

Although it is not as close to Leadbetter Point and Willapa Bay Wildlife Refuge as my previous offering, making base camp at Bruceport actually allows you to more fully explore all the nooks and crannies in and around this unique part of Pacific County.

The wildlife refuge headquarters is a good place to start, south on US 101 at mile marker 24 (a mile or so beyond the crossing of the Naselle River). It would be

MAP

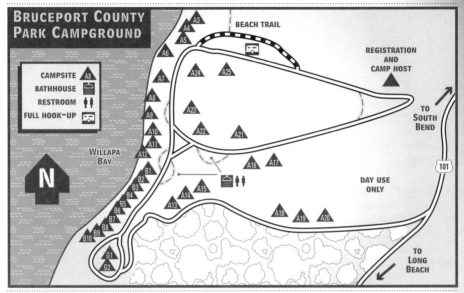

BRUCEPORT COUNTY PARK CAMPGROUND

BEACH TRAIL

REGISTRATION AND CAMP HOST

CAMPSITE	A8
BATHHOUSE	
RESTROOM	
FULL HOOK-UP	

TO SOUTH BEND

WILLAPA BAY

N

DAY USE ONLY

101

TO LONG BEACH

easy to spend your entire vacation educating yourself about the fragile, constantly shifting, wildlife-glutted wonders of this fascinating preserve. Definitely check out the newest addition at the headquarters—the Salmon Interpretive Trail with art installations created by University of Washington art students. If your interests lean more to local lore, head north to South Bend and visit the Pacific County Museum. Here, you'll find out why the history of Bruceport reads like a historical docudrama. If you just want to play, good destinations for beachcombing, kite flying, sea kayaking, and hiking surround you. Because this particular park does not have its own Web site and is given short shrift in most of the ones that mention it, the best sources I found for trip planning in this area were **www.funbeach.com** (Long Beach Peninsula Visitors Bureau) and **www.visit.willapabay.org** (Willapa Bay Organization).

GETTING THERE

From South Bend (approximately 30 miles south of Aberdeen), drive south 4 miles on US 101. The park entrance is on the right.

COHO CAMPGROUND

> *It's a long haul in, but the reward is a surprisingly natural setting on the banks of a man-made lake with many miles of trails to explore.*

RATINGS

Beauty: ✪ ✪ ✪ ✪ ✪
Privacy: ✪ ✪ ✪ ✪ ✪
Spaciousness: ✪ ✪ ✪ ✪ ✪
Quiet: ✪ ✪ ✪ ✪ ✪
Security: ✪ ✪ ✪
Cleanliness: ✪ ✪ ✪ ✪ ✪

WHEN THE FIRST form of life one encounters after driving roughly 35 miles on a lonely, tree-shrouded gravel-spewing Forest Service road is a group of red-headed (blood red, mind you) turkey vultures having a tête-à-tête in the middle of the road over last night's roadkill, one has to wonder if this is not some kind of significant omen. "I'd go back if I were you," to quote a road sign from the *Wizard of Oz*. I was feeling a bit like the Cowardly Lion.

Summoning up my c-c-c-courage, I stared those buzzards in the eye at about 10 paces (boy, are those things remarkably ugly and *big*) and asked in my most unintimidated voice, "Which way to Coho, fellas?"

Not much of a reply as they scattered to various tree stumps—watching me, the roadkill, and each other—and gave me the talons-up OK to pass. I didn't dally.

Much to my relief, I arrived at Coho shortly after this encounter and was shocked to find a fully functioning, well-developed campground on the prettily wooded shores of huge Wynoochee Lake. Outboards putt-putted out in the lake, campfire smells wafted through the trees, kids coasted by on bikes, squirrels scampered off with picnic table bounty. An Ozzie-and-Harriet camping scene, for sure. After my run-in with the redheads, I had pessimistically prepared myself for a scarred land, remnants of battered picnic tables, maybe a few deer carcasses hanging from the trees. You know, shades of how the approach to a witch's castle might look. The imagination plays amazing tricks when one travels alone. . . .

Particularly unexpected is the stretch of paved road that greets you just before the campground entrance. And takes you right up to the dam. Dam? Damn! There's a dam right next door!

Oh, well, if you can get beyond the presence of this less-than-natural edifice that supplies a portion of

Tacoma's power supply, the rest of the place is really quite natural. As if it feels we need convincing, the Forest Service maintains a Working Forest Nature Trail on the north side of the campground. It's hard to resist a peek at the overlook, even so. It comes complete with interpretive exhibits and views of the river gorge far below. There's a "fish collection" facility managed by Tacoma Power a few miles downriver from the dam if you're interested in the state of the species on the Wynoochee. Natural and man-made resources working together.

As for the campground, it's laid out in several loops under heavy forests with a total of 46 sites that are suited for tent campers, trailers, and RVs (although there are no hookups). You may prefer the walk-in sites. These struck me as afterthoughts, however. The standard sites offer lots of space and privacy, so if you have a choice, go for one of these. Spots on the lake are the most popular and go first, of course. But if you aren't early enough to be that lucky, don't fret. Most of the campers who come to Coho are weekenders with boats, and they'll be gone Sunday afternoon. Then, you'll have the place to yourself . . . just you and the vultures. Ha! Just kidding!

Actually, if you don't get lakeside accommodations, there's a nifty 16-mile trail where you can get your fill of lake views at every step. It follows the shoreline north to a bridge crossing on the Wynoochee River at 8 miles, then repeats the procedure on the far shore to bring you back across the dam to the campground. You can do either a one-way or retrace your steps. Probably too long for a day hike, but accessible via Forest Service Road 2270, is Wynoochee Falls. Not far beyond the falls but through a rather intricate series of Forest Service roads are the southern edges of Olympic National Park and the western access to Wonder Mountain Wilderness. These are relatively remote regions of these public lands and, as such, are likely to have crowd-free trails. Explore at will!

You may have already figured this out about Coho, but it's a long way from any commercial services, so make sure you've checked the checklist twice

KEY INFORMATION

ADDRESS: Coho
c/o Hood Canal
Ranger District
P.O. Box 68
150 North Lake
Cushman Road
Hoodsport, WA
98548

OPERATED BY: Olympic National Forest

INFORMATION: (360) 877-5254

OPEN: April–October

SITES: 56; 10 of which are walk-in tent sites; one of the walk-in sites can serve up to 12 people

EACH SITE HAS: Picnic tables, fire pit with grill

ASSIGNMENT: First come, first served

REGISTRATION: On site

FACILITIES: Restrooms with flush toilets; piped water; boat ramp; waste dump; garbage service; day-use area; public telephone

PARKING: At individual site and where designated for walk-in sites

FEE: $10 walk-in; $12 standard; $12 group walk-in

ELEVATION: 1,000 feet

RESTRICTIONS: Pets: On leash
Fires: In fire pits only
Alcohol: Permitted
Vehicles: Trailers and RVs up to 34 feet long
Other: No RV hookups

MAP

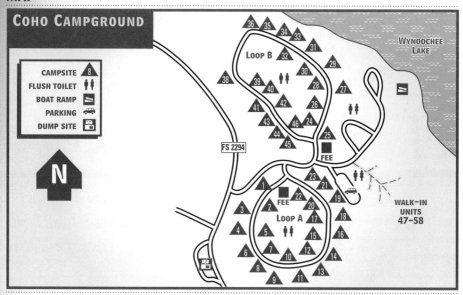

COHO CAMPGROUND

WYNOOCHEE LAKE

LOOP B

CAMPSITE
FLUSH TOILET
BOAT RAMP
PARKING
DUMP SITE

N

FS 2294

FEE

LOOP A

FEE

WALK-IN
UNITS
47-58

GETTING THERE

From Montesano on WA 12, turn north on Wynoochee Valley Road. Drive 35 miles (it becomes FS 22). At a main intersection, bear left to stay on FS 22. Within a half mile, turn right on FS 2294, and the campground is a mile in.

before you go. There *is* a pay telephone at the day-use area, which is great for things like calling a towing service if your car breaks down. But the chances of getting a pizza delivered are pretty slim!

COLLINS CAMPGROUND

WITH THE UNFORTUNATE closure of the upper portion of Dosewallips River Road in the fall of 2003, camping options up this lush valley have been pretty well obliterated until further notice. Web site information says that there are plans to begin rebuilding the road in 2005. The only problem is that the road will be built on the trail that currently goes around the washout and passes through old-growth forest. There is opposition to the notion of ruining old growth to reconnect less than a mile of roadway, so we'll see what happens.

Until then, one valley south of the Dosewallips is the Duckabush—equally unspoiled, with Collins Campground as a respectable replacement.

As with the Dosewallips, the Duckabush River drainage provided early settlers with a fertile base for farming, excellent timber for sturdy houses, and the shellfish bounty of Hood Canal nearby. The town of Brinnon, quietly established in 1860 by a handful of hardy souls, grew quickly around the turn of the century when word got out that a rail line between Hood Canal and Portland was in the works, which would make the area a booming logging concern.

The rail line did not materialize until much later, unfortunately. However, the beginnings of a managed forest began to appear at about the same time (1907), with the construction of the the first ranger cabin for the Olympic National Forest. Interrorem Guard Station was ranger-built and ranger-occupied up on the Duckabush, served throughout the century in various public-agency capacities, and remains in use today, having been somewhat modernized, as a recreational rental cabin. It is the oldest remaining building in the entire Olympic National Forest.

On that historical note, let's go camping. Up the road from the Interrorem Cabin sits Collins Camp-

> *Natural history and local legend commingle in an old-growth setting beside the Duckabush River.*

RATINGS

Beauty: ✰ ✰ ✰ ✰ ✰
Privacy: ✰ ✰ ✰ ✰ ✰
Spaciousness: ✰ ✰ ✰ ✰ ✰
Quiet: ✰ ✰ ✰ ✰ ✰
Security: ✰ ✰ ✰
Cleanliness: ✰ ✰ ✰ ✰ ✰

KEY INFORMATION

ADDRESS: Collins
c/o Hood Canal
Ranger District–
South
P.O. Box 68/
150 North Lake
Cushman Road
Hoodsport, WA
98548

OPERATED BY: Olympic National
Forest

INFORMATION: (360) 877-5254

OPEN: All year, weather
permitting (call in
off-season)

SITES: 16; 6 are tent-only

EACH SITE HAS: Picnic table, fire pit
with grill

ASSIGNMENT: First come, first
served

REGISTRATION: On site

FACILITIES: Vault toilets; piped
water within a half
mile

PARKING: At individual site

FEE: $10 per night
includes up to 2
vehicles; $5 each
additional vehicle

ELEVATION: 300 feet

RESTRICTIONS: Pets: On leash
Fires: In fire pits
only
Alcohol: Permitted
Vehicle: Trailers and
RVs up to 21 feet

ground. This could easily have been how things looked when the Civilian Conservation Corps (CCC) tramped around these parts back in the 1930s.

Collins is a classic Olympic National Forest beauty with giant old-growth fir and cedar interspersed with another common Olympic Peninsula dweller, the bigleaf maple. If you visit in the fall, you'll see why the bigleaf is renowned for its display of brilliant autumnal hues.

In keeping with the grandeur of the foliage, the campsites are generous in size (bordering on acreage) and there is generous space between each site. No contending with "camping claustrophobia" at Collins. Given the character of the land, every site is also beautifully flat (a feature often overlooked in modern campground design, but those CCC workers knew a thing or two). Natural undergrowth of salal, rhododendron, and swordfern define the boundaries of each site.

Aside from sites 3, 7, and 16 (which is where the last come, last served end up), all sites line the Duckabush River as it flows by at a pretty good rate, even late in the season. At high-water periods, it's not unthinkable that some of the campsites might get a little soggy around the edges. It was the decision of our camping committee (total votes: 2) that the best sites are 11, 12, and 14—factors used to weigh this conclusion included privacy, distance from parking, site size, and proximity to the river.

On an extraordinarily hot summer day in the Puget Sound basin (simmering in the mid-90s), the climate at Collins was just about perfect—shirtsleeve comfortable. The occupancy rate was a pleasant surprise, too. Only about half the sites were claimed on a Thursday afternoon, which leads me to think that—compared to other places I've been—Collins is a bit of a well-kept secret.

Primary activities in this part of the Olympic National Forest involve getting into the Olympic National Park, and the Duckabush Trail is designed to do just that. The trailhead is located about a mile west of the campground, and it can take you to points near and far, depending on your time frame and stamina. Collins is located just outside the access to The Brothers Wilderness—also worthy of exploration, with

MAP

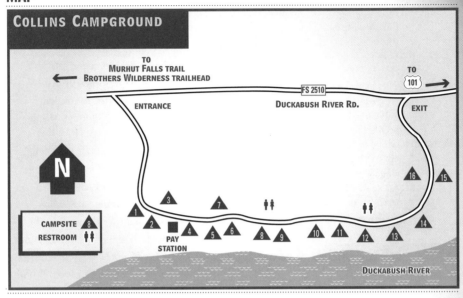

COLLINS CAMPGROUND

TO
MURHUT FALLS TRAIL
BROTHERS WILDERNESS TRAILHEAD

TO
101

FS 2510

DUCKABUSH RIVER RD.

ENTRANCE

EXIT

N

CAMPSITE 8
RESTROOM

PAY
STATION

DUCKABUSH RIVER

Mount Jupiter rising above its eastern boundary. Close enough for a quick morning rush is the drive and short hike up to Murhut Falls.

If you're in need of water (there is no potable water at Collins), here's an excuse to combine three activities in one: check out the Interrorem Interpretive Nature Trail (back beside the guard station), hike the Ranger Hole Trail down to the river (be cautious on the steep hillside and near the rapids here), and fill your water bottles at the faucet there on the way out!

The best autumn activity I can recommend is mushroom hunting (perfectly legal even without a permit, unless you plan to sell them). A source (who prefers to remain anonymous) says there is a to-die-for spot for chanterelles "somewhere" near the campground (applying a little bit of leg power). That's all I can tell you. Good luck!

GETTING THERE

From Hoodsport on the west side of Hood Canal, drive north 22 miles on US 101. Turn left (west) onto FS 2510 (Duckabush River Road) and drive 6 miles to the campground.

The camp access road is one-way, and the entrance is to the west of the exit.

From the north, take US 101 south from Quilcene for 15 miles, turn right onto FS 2510, and follow from there as above.

DEER PARK CAMPGROUND

A gem of a primitive, high-country bivouac inside the Olympic National Park with aerial-like views of the Olympic Range and alpine meadows.

THE SIGN READS, "Narrow winding road next 8 miles." OK, thanks for the warning. Frankly, I don't even remember seeing that sign on the way up. But I sure had a few words for it on the way out. Even took a picture to remind me.

Getting to Deer Park is kind of like applying for a government job. If you can get through the application, the job will be a breeze.

And that, Your Honor, is how I came to discover that I am a real chicken under certain backcountry road conditions.

Deer Park Road is definitely not for the faint of heart. Actually, the road condition is superb. Fine, smooth, graded gravel. Very few washboard ridges. No potholes. It's the altitude gain, the endless blind, hairpin, guardrail-challenged curves, the one-lane, I'm-over-as-far-as-I-can-go passages, and the sheer drop-offs that almost put me over the edge (pun fully intended). Possibly the longest 8 miles of nerve-racking driving that I've done. If you have any inclinations toward acrophobia or vertigo, let someone else drive. That's what I did on the way down. Thank you, Joan.

It's too bad I was so paralyzed on the way up because this 8 miles into the sky offers a new, stupendous view at every turn if you hit it on the kind of weekend we had. The entire Olympic Range lies before you as you momentarily burst out of the tree line. And you just know that if the scene is this good now, there's a possibility it might get better.

Which is exactly the case. Deer Park sits right at timberline just below the rounded summit of Blue Mountain and on the edge of glorious alpine meadows that simply shimmer in the hot August sun. A panoramic vista of razor-sharp mountain peaks, green valleys, and startling blue sky fill the eye. You find yourself taking deep breaths—partly from the rapid

RATINGS

Beauty: ✪ ✪ ✪ ✪ ✪
Privacy: ✪ ✪ ✪ ✪ ✪
Spaciousness: ✪ ✪ ✪ ✪ ✪
Quiet: ✪ ✪ ✪ ✪ ✪
Security: ✪ ✪ ✪ ✪ ✪
Cleanliness: ✪ ✪ ✪ ✪ ✪

altitude gain to 5,400 feet—of the woody, earthy fragrance that wild places like this emit.

You'll also find yourself squinting a lot in the brightness. This is a hat, sunglasses, and sunscreen zone. Bring plenty of water with you, too. Deer Park has no piped water.

The campground itself is a bit of an oddball assortment of haphazardly situated campsites in three separate loops wrapped around the southwest slope. Loops A and B are more exposed to the elements, with jumbles of weathered timber adorning their front yards and not a lot of privacy between sites. Loop C offers the most forested setting, but it's also the throughway to the very popular trailhead parking area and can be a bit busier than loops A and B.

We chose site 14 in loop C mainly because there weren't too many options at 6 p.m. on a Thursday in August. It turned out to be a delightful spot (despite being the closest to the trailhead parking), mostly because it's a large space, its focus is internal (with the tent space in the "lower forty"), and the trees provide considerable privacy.

The next morning we discovered the poorly marked site 13 straight across the parking lot from 14. We deduced that 13 is the best site in the camp, and that will be the choice on the next trip. It sits above the trailhead parking lot (which is where its parking space is, too), and a narrow trail through the meadow leads up to it. There is no campsite number marker as there are with the other sites. Site 13 is removed from the other campsites and affords the best blend of tree-line protection with views of flowered meadows. An added plus is a morning cup of coffee at the picnic table drenched in luscious sunlight. You may have day hikers visiting who think this is the trail to an outhouse, but you can direct them back to the toilet where the three loops intersect.

Activities at Deer Park range from knocking around on the numerous trails, to wildflower-identification sessions, to photo ops (when the quality of light presents itself), to nighttime stargazing, to an informative chat with a park ranger (the ranger station is on the spur road just below where Deer Park Road crests).

KEY INFORMATION

ADDRESS:	Deer Park c/o Olympic National Park 600 East Park Avenue Port Angeles, WA 98362-6798
OPERATED BY:	Olympic National Park
INFORMATION:	(360) 565-3130
OPEN:	Memorial Day through Labor Day
SITES:	15
EACH SITE HAS:	Picnic table, fire pit with grill
ASSIGNMENT:	First come, first served
REGISTRATION:	On site
FACILITIES:	Pit toilets; no piped water; ranger station nearby
PARKING:	At individual site
FEE:	$8
ELEVATION:	5,400 feet
RESTRICTIONS:	Pets: On leash Fires: In fire pits only Alcohol: Permitted Vehicles: Trailers and RVs not permitted Other: Firewood gathering prohibited

MAP

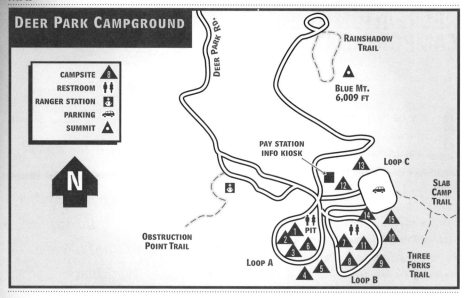

DEER PARK CAMPGROUND

CAMPSITE	8
RESTROOM	👫
RANGER STATION	🚹
PARKING	🚐
SUMMIT	▲

N

DEER PARK RD.

RAINSHADOW TRAIL

BLUE MT. 6,009 FT

PAY STATION INFO KIOSK

Loop C

SLAB CAMP TRAIL

OBSTRUCTION POINT TRAIL

PIT

LOOP A

THREE FORKS TRAIL

LOOP B

GETTING THERE

From Port Angeles, drive 6 miles east on US 101 to Deer Park Road. Turn right and follow this road 18 miles to the campground. The last 9 miles are smooth gravel but very steep, with blind hairpin turns and no guardrails. Be extremely careful on the curves, drive slowly, and honk if you're more comfortable announcing your presence. Better safe than sorry.

Wildlife viewing is pretty easy to do, too. Just sit in your campsite and watch the parade. We had a deer amble through several times while we were cooking dinner. A chipmunk boldly ransacked a bag of peanuts within seconds after we unpacked them. And those signs warning of bears? Take them seriously.

One last point: at this altitude, bring an extra layer even at the height of summer. Alpine nights are at least 10–15 °F colder than nights at sea level. Even on a day that peaked somewhere above 90, we were reaching for the fleece by the time the sun set and kept our socks on in the sleeping bags.

DUNGENESS RECREATION AREA CAMPGROUND

L ET ME TELL YOU about the day I almost didn't discover the rare beauty of Dungeness Recreation Area.

It was a hot and windy summer weekend. A friend and I had a late-afternoon, last-minute wild notion to hop a ferry across Puget Sound and take our bicycles with us. Destination: Dungeness Spit. We had been told that this was a special and unusual place, and we were eager to see firsthand if the description was deserved. We decided to explore by bicycle because the area is well suited to two-wheeled travel, with its flat, open expanses and pleasant country roads.

By midmorning the next day, we had battled our way by bicycle against a fierce headwind from where we had camped the night before (we didn't know about the campground at that point) to the park entrance. Windblown, we started down the narrow gravel road, following signs to the trailhead. Suddenly, an enormous automobile came careening up the road, filling up pretty much every usable inch of the lane and throwing up a shower of stones and cloud of dust behind it. Fortunately, it ground to a halt before smashing us up against the roadside vegetation. A head poked out the driver's-side window and a voice growled, "No sense goin' down there. Don't know what all the fuss is about. I didn't see nothin' special 'bout that place."

Well, this fellow must have seen some pretty amazing sights in his life to not have been impressed with Dungeness Spit, but I can tell you we were very glad we ignored his advice. We spent all afternoon exploring one of the supreme natural wonders of Washington State, and I'm sure I spent at least a week recovering from a delightful rare dose of too much sun and wind!

Dungeness Spit, the main attraction in the Dungeness Recreation Area/National Wildlife Refuge, is

> *This is the place from which to explore Dungeness Spit, one of the supreme natural wonders of Washington State.*

RATINGS

Beauty: ✿ ✿ ✿ ✿ ✿
Privacy: ✿ ✿ ✿ ✿ ✿
Spaciousness: ✿ ✿ ✿ ✿
Quiet: ✿ ✿ ✿ ✿
Security: ✿ ✿ ✿ ✿
Cleanliness: ✿ ✿ ✿ ✿

ADDRESS: Dungeness Recreation Area c/o Clallam County Parks Department 223 East Fourth Street Port Angeles, WA 98362

OPERATED BY: Clallam County Parks Department

INFORMATION: (360) 683-5847

OPEN: February 1–October 1

SITES: 65

EACH SITE HAS: Picnic table, fire pit, shade trees

ASSIGNMENT: First come, first served; no reservations

REGISTRATION: At park information booth from daylight to dusk

FACILITIES: Bathhouse with sinks, toilets, showers, hot water; public telephone; playground; firewood (for a small fee)

PARKING: At individual sites

FEE: $12 per night for Clallam County residents; $14 for non-residents

ELEVATION: Sea level

RESTRICTIONS: **Pets:** On leash; no dogs on beach
Fires: In fire pits only
Alcohol: Prohibited
Vehicles: No limit on RV or trailer size

the longest natural sand spit in the United States. Arcing nearly 7 miles into the Strait of Juan de Fuca on the Olympic Peninsula, this unique landform averages only 100 yards wide for its entire length. Its outer (western) shore faces the open surf and uninterrupted winds of the strait that cause driftwood to collect in jumbled masses like piles of giant bones.

The inner shore—with smaller Graveyard Spit protruding from it—marks the boundary of Dungeness Bay. The innermost shoreline of this bay—actually an extremely shallow lagoon formed by Graveyard's finger—beckons thousands of migratory and wintering shorebirds that rest on the lush vegetation that flourishes in these marshlike conditions. The oldest inland lighthouse in Washington sits a half mile from the spit's end and warns off passing ships that can easily miscalculate their distance from barely submerged shoals.

The entire expanse of spits, tidelands, wetlands, landmarks, and adjoining surf forms Dungeness National Wildlife Refuge. While jurisdiction of the refuge belongs to the U.S. Department of Fish & Wildlife, Dungeness Recreation Area is in the hands of the Clallam County Parks Department. It is the largest of nine facilities managed by the county agency, most of which make use of the saltwater northern peninsula in some fashion.

The Dungeness Recreation Area campsites are well designed around two loops, affording ultimate privacy with dense undergrowth between sites. About a third of the sites are spaced along a high bluff that overlooks the Strait of Juan de Fuca and offer million-dollar views for the mere price of a campsite. On a clear night, look across to the twinkling lights of Victoria, British Columbia's capital, on the southern tip of Vancouver Island. Depending on the season and your timing, you may be able to enjoy this view complete with a dinner of world-famous Dungeness crab, caught in the local waters and cooked on your campstove. Check with the Sequim chamber of commerce for information on where to find fresh local crab.

Chances are you'll have more spectacular views than not—this area of the Olympic Peninsula lies within the rainshadow of the Olympic Mountains and, as a

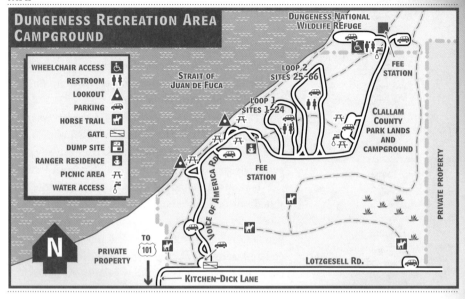

result, receives far less rain than just about any other area of western Washington. Rainfall averages about 15 inches per year (compared to Seattle's 35–50).

Despite the moderate year-round climate, the campground is open only from February 1 to October 1. Summer can be quite busy, so you may want to try the off-season.

In addition to the ever-popular beachcombing, park activities include horseback riding (using a separate equestrian trail and unloading area), gamebird hunting in designated areas, and good old-fashioned picnicking along the bluff, with its stunning view.

GETTING THERE

From Sequim, drive 5 miles west on US 101 to Kitchen–Dick Lane. Turn north (right) and drive 3 miles, watching for signs to the recreation area campground and entrance. The entrance is on the left just past the 90-degree turn where Kitchen–Dick becomes Lotzgesell Road.

HOH RAIN FOREST CAMPGROUND

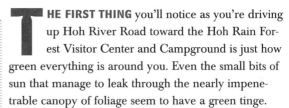

> *One of only three temperate rain forests in the world, this is a unique and therefore popular destination, especially with hikers. You may want to visit in the off-season.*

RATINGS

Beauty: ✮ ✮ ✮ ✮ ✮
Privacy: ✮ ✮ ✮ ✮
Spaciousness: ✮ ✮ ✮ ✮
Quiet: ✮ ✮ ✮ ✮
Security: ✮ ✮ ✮
Cleanliness: ✮ ✮ ✮ ✮ ✮

THE FIRST THING you'll notice as you're driving up Hoh River Road toward the Hoh Rain Forest Visitor Center and Campground is just how green everything is around you. Even the small bits of sun that manage to leak through the nearly impenetrable canopy of foliage seem to have a green tinge.

The second thing you'll notice is the pale gray-green shrouds of mosses and lichens that drape ghoulishly from tree branches. The weight of these hangers-on often causes limbs to snap under the stress.

Third, as you stand amid the hushed majesty of this primeval forest, you'll notice the most insidious and perpetual characteristic of a temperate rain forest— the steady *plink! plink! plink!* as droplet after droplet of moisture makes its small but significant contribution to this fascinating, self-sustaining ecosystem.

The Hoh Rain Forest is only one of three temperate rain forests in the entire world. It has had the good fortune to have remained in its original state for thousands of years, thanks to the vision of a few men around the turn of the century who recommended the preservation of the Roosevelt elk habitat. Their efforts led first to the creation of the Olympic Forest Reserve, then to Mount Olympus National Monument (under Teddy Roosevelt), and finally to Olympic National Park (under Franklin Roosevelt).

You will notice as you make your way around Olympic Peninsula to the Hoh entrance that logging has been rampant up to the park boundary. Examples of the colossal trees that once blanketed the western slopes of the Olympic Mountains all the way to the coast have, fortunately, been preserved within the park's borders. Four of the nine world record holders are along the Hoh River and its forks. Check with the visitor center for their exact locations.

The Hoh Rain Forest Visitor Center and Campground will probably be one of the busiest facilities you'll come across in this book. The rain forest attracts visitors from all over the world, but its uniqueness warrants inclusion in this car-camping guide. Summer sees the most visitors, naturally, but the visitor center and campground are open year-round, so you may want to plan a visit in the off-season.

Temperatures are never really hot or cold at any time of the year in the Hoh Valley, but spending time here in seasons other than summer and late spring means limiting your hiking to low elevations. The Hoh River Valley itself is a grand off-season walk, with round-trip distances up to 18 miles without significant altitude gain. In the immediate vicinity of the visitor center are three short nature trails of varying lengths that feature fine examples of rain forest vegetation. One often sees elk on these short trips.

For the more energetic backpackers who come to the Hoh in summer, Hoh River Trail is the most popular access to Mount Olympus (mainly because it is the shortest way in from a road-end). It's 18.5 miles to Blue Glacier at the base of the east peak of Mount Olympus. The Hoh trail also connects with other major (trunk) trails in the park. Backcountry permits are required for any overnight travel on trails. Check with a park ranger for further information if you plan extended backpack trips within the park. The nearest spot for supplies is Westward Hoh (5.6 miles from the intersection with US 101).

You are advised not to attempt boating or swimming in the Hoh River because it moves rapidly and is very cold and often jammed with logs. Fishing is, however, one safe option, and a list of regulations is available at the visitor center.

The campground is set between two bends in the river, giving campers the most river frontage possible. The best sites will be those in loops A and C that are closest to the river. Unless the river is at flood stage, just sitting and watching the flow of water can, in itself, be a mesmerizing and soothing activity. If the river floods, there's a good chance you won't even get this far up the road. There are ongoing efforts to keep the

KEY INFORMATION

ADDRESS: Hoh Rain Forest Campground Hoh Rain Forest Visitor Center c/o Olympic National Park Port Angeles, WA 98362

OPERATED BY: Hoh Ranger Station, Olympic National Park, National Park Service, U.S. Department of Interior

INFORMATION: (360) 374-6925, ranger station; (360) 452-4501, park headquarters

OPEN: All year

SITES: 88

EACH SITE HAS: Fire grill, picnic table

ASSIGNMENT: First come, first served; no reservations

REGISTRATION: Self-registration at bulletin board next to restrooms

FACILITIES: Piped water; restrooms with flush toilets, sinks, disabled access; animal-proof storage lockers; RV dump station; summer naturalist program; visitor center

PARKING: At individual sites

FEE: $10 per night

ELEVATION: 578 feet

RESTRICTIONS: Pets: On leash at all times; not allowed on trails or in public buildings
Fires: In fire pits
Alcohol: Permitted
Vehicles: RVs up to 21 feet; no hookups
Other: Do not feed birds or animals; permits required for overnight hikes

MAP

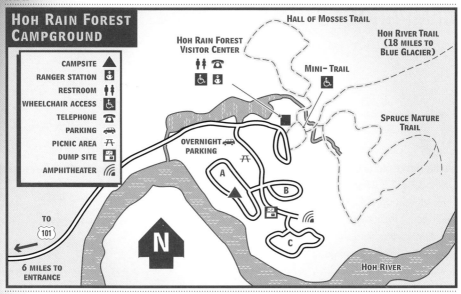

HOH RAIN FOREST CAMPGROUND

CAMPSITE	▲
RANGER STATION	
RESTROOM	⋔⋔
WHEELCHAIR ACCESS	♿
TELEPHONE	☎
PARKING	🚗
PICNIC AREA	⊼
DUMP SITE	
AMPHITHEATER	📶

HALL OF MOSSES TRAIL

HOH RAIN FOREST VISITOR CENTER

HOH RIVER TRAIL (18 MILES TO BLUE GLACIER)

MINI-TRAIL

SPRUCE NATURE TRAIL

OVERNIGHT PARKING

A

B

C

TO 101

N

6 MILES TO ENTRANCE

HOH RIVER

GETTING THERE

From north or south, take US 101 around the Olympic Peninsula to the west side of Olympic National Park. Turn east onto Upper Hoh Road about 18 miles south of the town of Forks; the campground is at the end of the road. The driving distance from Seattle by way of Olympia is roughly 200 miles. By way of Washington State ferries to Winslow or Kingston, the road distance is about 145 miles. Ferry crossings take about half an hour.

slides and washouts to a minimum. In the summer of 2004 a monstrous sum of money was appropriated to keep the rambunctious Hoh from ruining the road system along it.

It's worth noting that the drive to the Hoh River Valley is easily several hours by car from metropolitan Puget Sound. Unless you already plan to be on the peninsula, this is a long weekend outing.

LYRE RIVER CAMPGROUND

OBSCURED BY THE CLAMOR for the Sol Duc River, Lake Crescent, Neah Bay, Lake Ozette, the Black Ball Ferry to Victoria, Salt Creek Recreation Area—you name it—the Lyre River Campground is another one of those Department of Natural Resources (DNR) hidden gems that has everything going for it and nobody promoting it—until now.

For starters, and thanks to the generous contribution of the DNR (although this could change very soon), it's free. Second, it's an agate's throw from the pebble-strewn beaches of the Strait of Juan de Fuca. Third, it's just far enough outside the Olympic National Park radar to get conveniently overlooked. Plus, it is easily confused with the Lyre River Park (a privately run resort that must have spent every extra dollar they made to get written up in just about every guidebook and on every Web site that lists recreational accommodations on the north Olympic Peninsula). Finally, the Lyre River at its origins with Lake Crescent happens to be home to a species of trout that is found *nowhere else on Earth!*

Ha! How's that for a heavy-hitting package?

Need still more enticement? OK, how about this one? Sounds like a fish tale to me, but what the heck! Puts a bit of romance and civility into the place. Local lore has it that early settlers from the East who found themselves homesick for Carnegie Hall (that part may be a stretch) dubbed it "lyre" because the sound of the water playing over the stones was reminiscent of a nubile, scantily clad young Indian maiden (that might be even more of a stretch) plucking the strings of a lyre.

Truthfully, an interpretive sign at the park explains the origin of both the river's and, ultimately, the campground's, name. Am I exaggerating by much? I think not!

> *Free camping on the Olympic Peninsula is almost unheard of, but here's one that is also far enough off the beaten path and only a short distance from salt water.*

RATINGS

Beauty: ✪ ✪ ✪
Privacy: ✪ ✪ ✪ ✪
Spaciousness: ✪ ✪ ✪ ✪
Quiet: ✪ ✪ ✪ ✪
Security: ✪ ✪ ✪
Cleanliness: ✪ ✪ ✪ ✪ ✪

ADDRESS: Lyre River
Campground
c/o Olympic Region
411 Tillicum Lane
Forks, WA
98331-9271

OPERATED BY: Washington State
Department of
Natural Resources

INFORMATION: (360) 374-6131

OPEN: All year

SITES: 11

EACH SITE HAS: Picnic table, fire pit
with grill

ASSIGNMENT: First come, first
served

REGISTRATION: Not necessary

FACILITIES: Vault toilets; piped
water; picnic shelter
with fireplace

PARKING: At individual site

FEE: No fee

ELEVATION: Sea level

RESTRICTIONS: Pets: On leash
Fires: In fire pits
only
Alcohol: Permitted
Vehicles: Trailers
and RVs not recom-
mended

On to more serious matters. Like camping.

Nestled in private pockets of Olympic coastal veg-etation, each of the 11 campsites at Lyre River are close enough to the river for one to hear and hum along with its melody. The DNR has not outdone itself with elaborate upgrades, and all is maintained in a very natural state (read: primitive). There is a picnic shelter identical to every one I've seen at other DNR sites. Probably most uncharacteristic for a DNR site is the presence of piped water—an amenity you come to not expect, but are pleasantly surprised to find, in rus-tic surroundings.

There is no doubt that Lyre's main allure is its coastal location providing saltwater access. Rock col-lecting and tidepool marveling could keep you busy all day. But eventually the tide rushes in and, unless you like getting very wet, you'll have to find alternative entertainment.

This calls for some upland meandering. There's a destination in every direction, but some of the more notable ascents (and easily managed in a few hours) are Striped Peak Lookout—over at Salt Creek Recre-ation Area, Spruce Railroad Trail—hugging Lake Cres-cent's north shore, and the more challenging Mount Storm King summit that rises high above Lake Cres-cent on the Olympic National Park boundary.

As noted early on, the headwaters of the Lyre at Lake Crescent are, for reasons unknown, the singular spawning ground for the prized Beardslee rainbow trout. The fate of this rare species that is native only to Lake Crescent has come under the scrutiny of Washington Trout (essentially a well-intentioned nonprofit fish-police organization) in the past several years. At its urging, the national park has agreed to a catch-and-release-only pro-gram as the first critical step in saving the fish. This puts Lyre River on the map, so to speak, for anglers who pay attention to these kinds of developments. To most fisher-men, however, and fortunately for the Beardslee rain-bow, the Lyre is popular for its salmon and steelhead runs. The campground obliges with an area that accom-modates the activity accordingly.

For all its primitiveness, Lyre River embraces a barrier-free principle, with one campsite, all facilities,

MAP

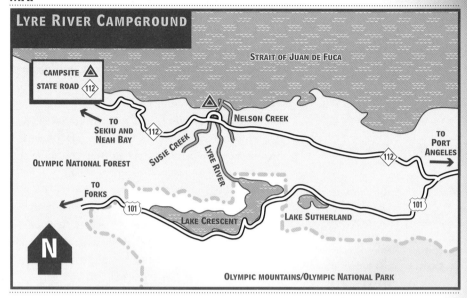

LYRE RIVER CAMPGROUND

CAMPSITE △
STATE ROAD ⟨112⟩

STRAIT OF JUAN DE FUCA

TO SEKIU AND NEAH BAY

NELSON CREEK

TO PORT ANGELES

SUSIE CREEK
LYRE RIVER

OLYMPIC NATIONAL FOREST

TO FORKS

LAKE CRESCENT

LAKE SUTHERLAND

N

OLYMPIC MOUNTAINS/OLYMPIC NATIONAL PARK

the parking lot, and the path that leads to the campsite all wheelchair accessible. Between this accommodation of the challenged recreationist and the efforts being made to restore the endangered trout population, we can be proud that public agencies are taking this kind of initiative even in such low-impact areas as Lyre River.

It's enough to make me want to strum a tune. Now where did I put my lyre?

GETTING THERE

From Port Angeles, go west on US 101 roughly 5 miles to the turn for WA 112 (Sekiu/Neah Bay). Then head west on WA 112 and look for Lyre River Road (paved) between mileposts 46 and 47. Turn right, drive a half mile, and turn left into the campground. Don't confuse this campground with the privately owned and operated Lyre River Resort and RV Park. The private resort is farther west on West Lyre River Road and has signage that can be misleading.

MORA CAMPGROUND

> *No other public campground in Washington State brings you so close by car to wilderness beaches that are accessible only by foot both north and south.*

GRAB YOUR **GORE-TEX** for this one! We're heading for the wet and wild (or, should I say, wetter and wilder?) side of Olympic National Park to some of the last stretches of coastal wilderness left in the contiguous United States.

Mora Campground, part of the network of well-attended Olympic National Park facilities, is among the elite when it comes to its location only a mile or so from the Pacific Ocean. For a total of 57 unspoiled and challenging miles (from the Quillayute River north to the boundary of the Makah Indian Reservation, and south to the legendary Hoh River and its namesake tribal grounds), the saltwater frontage of the Pacific Ocean features numerous protruding headlands, swirling tidepools, crashing surf, and stalwart "sea-stacks."

For many years, this outpost of civilization was an active trading port up the Quillayute River for ships from Seattle. When neither roads nor rail materialized, boat-only access kept Mora safe from further development.

In 1990 a major oil spill near Cape Flattery (the northwesternmost piece of land in the lower 48 states) cast a pall over certain sections of the coastal parklands. It will never be the same, but the latest reports seem to indicate that much of the oil was controlled and scooped up, thanks to the quick response of various agencies.

Fortunately, this is still one of the truly remarkable and entrancing spots in the country, perhaps even in the world. The blend of natural geography, cultural influence, and historical record are a powerful combination. The weather-beaten Washington coast can be formidable even when there are no storms. This is a place where rain slickers, wool sweaters, waterproof footwear, and a hat you can hold onto are very much in order any time of the year. Western winds hit the coast

RATINGS

Beauty: ✪ ✪ ✪ ✪ ✪
Privacy: ✪ ✪ ✪ ✪
Spaciousness: ✪ ✪ ✪ ✪ ✪
Quiet: ✪ ✪ ✪ ✪ ✪
Security: ✪ ✪ ✪
Cleanliness: ✪ ✪ ✪ ✪

unchecked and work the surf into a foaming frenzy. As a result, the shape of the coastline is forever changing.

Mora Campground is a relatively large complex compared with other Olympic Park accommodations. Situated at sea level, Mora is open all year and is an ideal choice for off-season travel. Actually, winter and early spring can be some of the best times, weather-wise, to be on the Washington coast. You'll have an opportunity to watch the migratory gray whales that pass on their way to southern California and Mexico.

The campground is comprised of five loops. Sites are so spacious among the giant firs and cedars and shrouded from each other by the dense, low-growing foliage that even at its busiest, Mora offers campers side-by-side solitude. Only the most monstrous RVs poke out from their parking spaces in what seems like embarrassed apology.

If time allows, be sure to take the full tour of all the loops before deciding on your site. You may want to park and enjoy the tour on foot. This will give you the best sense of the place and a good firsthand analysis of where you're going to make your home for the next few days. Plus, the grandeur of the land loses something with motor vehicles puttering around. It's too bad there isn't some system to shuttle campers in and out of Mora by boat, long canoe, or Indian pony. These seem much more fitting modes of travel here.

Since Mora is first come, first served (like most of the developed campgrounds in Olympic National Park), the best sites will fill up fast—but in this camp-ground, the definition of "best" may depend on the camper. My first choice would be any of the sites in loop E on the river side. But perhaps the best site in the entire campground is what used to be the group camp. Severe flooding has restructured the site to walk-in only; it can accommodate up to six people (two tents maximum). It sits alone at the end of loop D on a low bluff above the Quillayute surrounded by trees and shrubbery. The walk is down a wide, well-maintained path that was softened with fresh cedar chips when I was there.

Ocean access from Mora is two miles beyond the campground at Rialto Beach, where there is ample

KEY INFORMATION

ADDRESS: Mora Campground c/o Mora Ranger Station 3283 Mora Road Forks, WA 98331

OPERATED BY: Olympic National Park, National Park Service, U.S. Department of the Interior

INFORMATION: (360) 374-5460

OPEN: All year

SITES: 94; 1 walk-in

EACH SITE HAS: Fire grill, picnic table

ASSIGNMENT: First come, first served; no reservations

REGISTRATION: Self-registration on site

FACILITIES: Bathhouse with toilets, sinks, running water, drinking water, disabled access

PARKING: At individual sites

FEE: $10 per night

ELEVATION: Sea level

RESTRICTIONS: Pets: On leash Fires: In fire pits Alcohol: Permitted Vehicles: RVs up to 21 feet; no vehicles allowed off park roads Other: Permits required for extended hikes into backcountry

MAP

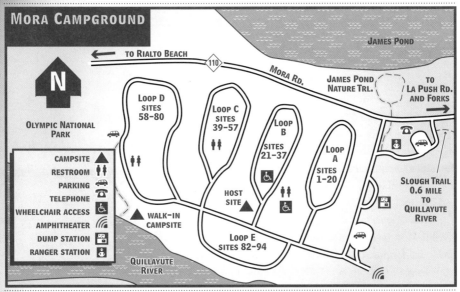

MORA CAMPGROUND

JAMES POND

TO RIALTO BEACH

110

MORA RD.

JAMES POND NATURE TRL.

TO LA PUSH RD. AND FORKS

N

LOOP D
SITES
58-80

LOOP C
SITES
39-57

LOOP B

OLYMPIC NATIONAL PARK

SITES 21-37

LOOP A

SITES 1-20

SLOUGH TRAIL
0.6 MILE
TO
QUILLAYUTE
RIVER

CAMPSITE	▲
RESTROOM	🚻
PARKING	🚐
TELEPHONE	☎
WHEELCHAIR ACCESS	♿
AMPHITHEATER	🎦
DUMP STATION	🚽
RANGER STATION	🛈

HOST SITE ▲

WALK-IN CAMPSITE ▲

LOOP E
SITES 82-94

QUILLAYUTE RIVER

GETTING THERE

Whether from north or south, take US 101 around the Olympic Peninsula to the town of Forks (between 125 and 200 miles from Seattle, depending on which route you take). About 1 mile north of Forks, turn west onto La Push Road and drive for about 10 miles to Mora Road. Turn right onto Mora Road and follow the signs to the campground.

parking for a day hike or an extended trek. Permits are required if you plan to stay on the wilderness beach overnight. A word of warning: coastal hiking requires a tide table at all times of the year. Many of the points, bluffs, heads, and capes are covered at high tide, and you'll need to either wait out the tide or, where possible, go overland to continue. Even the inland routes can be muddy and treacherous, so make sure you have good traction on your shoes or boots. The "Strip of Wilderness" brochure available at the Mora Ranger Station is full of information about the pleasures and pitfalls of coastal hiking.

Check at either the Mora station or information stations along US 101—there's one north of Forks and one at Kalaloch—for other options in this part of Olympic National Park and the surrounding national forest.

One last word: the Indian reservations that border the park along the coast are private lands. Be respectful of this fact.

UPPER CLEARWATER CAMPGROUND

FOR SHEER ESCAPISM, it's hard to beat Upper Clearwater. I'll get blasted for saying this, but there may be only one other campground on the entire Olympic Peninsula in a more remote setting that is accessible by automobile. That's Yahoo Lake, and it's right up the road from Upper Clearwater.

These Department of Natural Resources (DNR) "facilities" (it seems like a stretch to identify them as such), are for purist, minimalist tent campers. Remember minimal? OK, quick refresher: as close to a wilderness experience as possible, preferably geared more to tent camping than RVs, and scenic.

Upper Clearwater meets all three criteria—and goes no further. In truth, I was unable to visit Upper Clearwater after the floods of 2003, so I haven't been there since summer 2002 and can't say from personal experience exactly what the condition of the campground is at the moment. But the last information I had from the DNR was that it is open, so it must have withstood the floods better than other areas.

Hopefully, it's still as I remember it and remains one of those best-kept secrets (allowing for the masses that will discover it through this book, of course), a place for getting the heck away from everything in a rain forest–style setting beside a river that lives up to its name.

There are nine sites, all thickly shrouded in Olympic Forest vegetation and most on the river. Each comes with the standard-issue picnic table and fire pit with grill. Aside from a pit toilet, the only other obvious man-made contribution is a handy shelter that could be highly desirable if you hit a particularly wet weekend. Those DNR folks think of everything!

There's also a very primitive boat put-in spot (for hand-carried and human-powered boats only). Frankly, at this stage in the river's progress, it's difficult to imag-

> *This refreshingly simple campground offers solitude to contrast with the overrun parts of the Olympic Peninsula.*

RATINGS

Beauty: ✩ ✩ ✩ ✩
Privacy: ✩ ✩ ✩ ✩ ✩
Spaciousness: ✩ ✩ ✩
Quiet: ✩ ✩ ✩ ✩ ✩
Security: ✩ ✩ ✩
Cleanliness: ✩ ✩ ✩ ✩ ✩

ADDRESS: Upper Clearwater
c/o Olympic Region
411 Tillicum Lane
Forks, WA
98331-9797

OPERATED BY: Washington State
Department of
Natural Resources

INFORMATION: (360) 374-6131

OPEN: All year

SITES: 9

EACH SITE HAS: Picnic table, fire pit
with grill

ASSIGNMENT: First come, first
served

REGISTRATION: Not necessary

FACILITIES: Vault toilets; shelter;
hand boat launch;
nonpotable water;
no garbage service

PARKING: At individual site

FEE: No fee

ELEVATION: 900 feet

RESTRICTIONS: **Pets:** On leash
Fires: In fire pits
only
Alcohol: Permitted
Vehicles: Small trailers only (limited side
clearance)

ine floating anything much larger than a rubber ducky. From its origins off an unnamed ridge just outside the Olympic National Park boundary not more than 15 miles from Upper Clearwater, the river is still fairly narrow, taking a lot of sharp turns and dropping fast while not widening much. Not until it picks up the added support of numerous feeder creeks does its flow move obviously into the river category. Keep in mind, however, that my visit was well into one of the driest summers on record, so spring and early summer runoff may prove greater at higher elevations.

In fact, the Clearwater warrants mention as a decent Class I paddle stream in various books on the subject. The suggested put-in spot is at the bridge crossing (about 7 miles downriver from Upper Clearwater) with the takeout at the DNR picnic spot about 2 miles before you get to US 101. The total run is roughly 11 miles.

For higher-elevation pursuits, the area around Yahoo Lake is ripe for exploration, with hiking trails on surrounding slopes and good fishing in the lake. This is a drive-to, hike-in, end-of-road option and also a respectable camping spot (if portaging camping supplies is up your alley). Campsites are about 150 yards from the parking area (which isn't an unmanageable distance), but it is advised to put all food items or other highly odorous effects you may have with you in the car at night to avoid piquing the interest of marauding bears. This is, after all, wilderness by definition if not by designation.

It's very curious that, with all the national forest and national park lands that abound on the Olympic Peninsula, the Clearwater corridor remains in DNR hands. My impression of the DNR is that they are stewards of public lands that have not only commercial (a.k.a. exploitable) value, but also unique characteristics deserving protection. This is an odd dichotomy, but perhaps one not unexpected. Lands on the Olympic Peninsula once fostered job security through logging and fishing, but now, with those industries floundering, are gradually shifting to recreational usage.

As such, Upper Clearwater and its fellow DNR facilities in the area (namely Coppermine Bottom

MAP

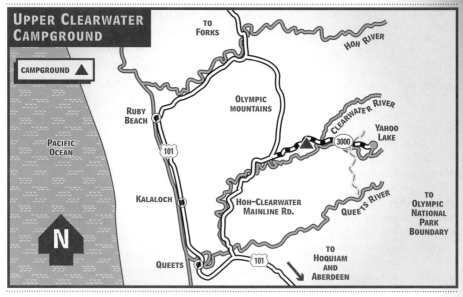

UPPER CLEARWATER
CAMPGROUND

CAMPGROUND ▲

TO
FORKS

HOH RIVER

OLYMPIC
MOUNTAINS

RUBY
BEACH

CLEARWATER RIVER

YAHOO
LAKE

3000

PACIFIC
OCEAN

101

KALALOCH

HOH–CLEARWATER
MAINLINE RD.

QUEETS RIVER

TO
OLYMPIC
NATIONAL
PARK
BOUNDARY

N

QUEETS

101

TO
HOQUIAM
AND
ABERDEEN

farther down the Clearwater) perhaps enjoy a more hands-off management style than the more regulated and heavily promoted facilities of the National Park Service and the National Forest Service.

Enjoy it while it lasts. And thank the DNR for the ability to access a classic temperate rainforest setting (complete with its own old growth examples) in an understated fashion.

GETTING THERE

From Queets, drive south on US 101 for about 5 miles to the Hoh–Clearwater Mainline Road. Turn left, crossing the Queets River, and travel 13 paved miles to C-3000 Road. Turn right and continue 3.2 graveled, narrow miles to the campground on the right.

PUGET **SOUND**

BOWMAN BAY/ DECEPTION PASS STATE PARK CAMPGROUND

WASHINGTON STATE PARKS are seldom escapes from the crowds, and Deception Pass State Park is no exception to this. They are, however, almost always delightful escapes from the ordinary, and Deception Pass reigns supreme in this department.

Anchored on both sides of the body of water that separates Whidbey Island from Fidalgo Island, Deception Pass State Park literally offers something for everybody—even us tent campers. Although believing that you might find yourself alone at any point during the summer season is insane, this area is so appealing that in deference to the tent-camping mandate of this book, I must include it.

I gave serious thought to nixing it when I visited the park several times during the summer of 2004, but I kept coming back to the fact that it's too damned spectacular! I can't help it if lots of other people think so, too.

However, there is a portion of the park that seems to be largely overlooked. It could be the signage (or lack thereof) that causes a problem. (Whatever it is, I'm not tellin' when I find out!) Given this, let's explore the tent-camping attributes of one of the most popular state parks on the planet.

First, the section of campsites on the north side of the park (the Fidalgo Island side) number only 16 (compared to 230 in the Whidbey Island sector). Don't be confused by the fact that they are numbered 236 through 251 and are reservable (highly recommended if you can plan ahead a few months for the peak season).

Second, the sites themselves are obviously geared toward tent camping. The camp road is narrow, it follows the somewhat hilly contour of the bulk of Rosario Head on which it sits, the parking spurs are tight, there are no hookups, and the sites are decently spaced, with

> *This is the less overrun part of Deception Pass State Park, tucked away in a saltwater bayside setting with historical significance.*

RATINGS

Beauty: ✪ ✪ ✪ ✪ ✪
Privacy: ✪ ✪ ✪
Spaciousness: ✪ ✪ ✪
Quiet: ✪ ✪ ✪ ✪
Security: ✪ ✪ ✪
Cleanliness: ✪ ✪ ✪ ✪ ✪

ADDRESS: Bowman Bay/ Deception Pass State Park 41229 North WA 20 Oak Harbor, WA 98277

OPERATED BY: Washington State Parks and Recreation Commission

INFORMATION: (360) 902-8844; www.parks.wa.gov

OPEN: All year; some campsites closed in winter

SITES: 16 tent sites

EACH SITE HAS: Picnic table, fire pit with grill

ASSIGNMENT: Reservations accepted up to 9 months in advance; recommended during peak season; reservations at (888) CAMPOUT or www.parks.wa.gov, otherwise first come, first served

FACILITIES: Restrooms (ADA) with showers; picnic area; historical interpretive center; boat launch; fishing pier

PARKING: At individual site

FEE: $16; second vehicle $10

ELEVATION: Sea level

RESTRICTIONS: Pets: On leash Fires: In fire pits only; no wood gathering Alcohol: In designated areas; no kegs Vehicles: Sites not suitable for trailer parking

generous undergrowth between each. The general sense of the place is one of intimate and uncluttered relaxation in a very natural state—the absence of RVs (with the exception of the camp host parked at the outermost space on the outbound end of the loop) helps. Compare this to the crush of campsites with pull-throughs and hookups over on Whidbey Island, and you will be back here in a flash.

The geography further aids in promoting this sector of the park as the domain of tent campers and a more simplified—dare I say more dignified?—park experience. Bowman Bay's silky, protected waters within the curve of the shoreline glisten before you. Views of headlands covered with weather-beaten madronas and evergreens contrast directly with the sandy shoreline at your feet. A former bathhouse built by the Civilian Conservation Corps back in the 1930s has been restored and serves as an interpretive center, lending its own time-worn quality to the scene. Tucked into the hillside above the camp road, the ranger's quaint quarters complete the picture-postcard setting.

A look at the statistics of this magnificent park will quickly lead you to conclude that exploring its sprawling environs is a must—and it is best done by foot, bike, or boat. For starters, the park encompasses 4,134 acres. There are 38 miles of hiking trails, 77,000 feet of saltwater frontage, and 33,900 feet of fresh water divided among four lakes. Boats have 710 feet of saltwater dock access, 1,980 feet of saltwater moorage, and 450 feet of freshwater dock. There are wetlands, sand dunes, interpretive trails, Native American stories, historical monuments, a saltwater fishing pier, and an astonishing array of wildlife, sea life, and birds. If that's not enough to keep you busy for at least a week of vacation, sit in on a weekend ranger program at one of the two amphitheaters and see what you missed.

For all that Deception Pass State Park has to offer, I feel compelled to lodge one small complaint. Granted, the bridge that connects the parts of this remarkable area is one hell of an engineering marvel, and the views from it are unequalled. But I have never understood the logic behind allowing

MAP

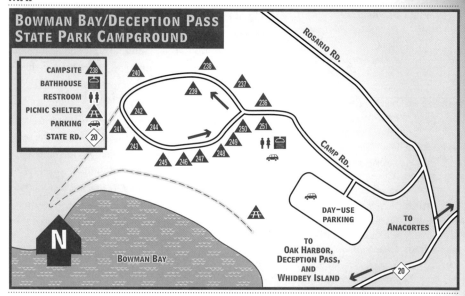

**BOWMAN BAY/DECEPTION PASS
STATE PARK CAMPGROUND**

CAMPSITE	238
BATHHOUSE	
RESTROOM	
PICNIC SHELTER	
PARKING	
STATE RD.	20

ROSARIO RD.

240 238 237 239 236 242 241 244 250 251 243 249 248 245 246 247

CAMP RD.

DAY-USE
PARKING

TO
ANACORTES

N

BOWMAN BAY

TO
OAK HARBOR,
DECEPTION PASS,
AND
WHIDBEY ISLAND

20

---

pedestrians to wander along what is often a windswept or fogbound catwalk with major traffic whizzing by. Gives me the willies!

GETTING THERE

From Anacortes, drive 9 miles south on WA 20. Turn right onto Rosario Road then make an immediate left (and I mean *immediate*) onto the camp access road at the sign for Bowman Bay. Drive down the cool, forested lane and continue straight beyond the sign for the boat launch to the camping loop.

DASH POINT STATE PARK CAMPGROUND

If you've just flown in to the Seattle–Tacoma area with your backpack, campstove, and tent roll and you want to make a quick escape, relief is just moments away.

LOCATED ON THE SHORE of Puget Sound only 6 miles north of Tacoma and 20 miles south of Seattle, Dash Point State Park is 400 acres of lush privacy and sandy coastline complemented by modern facilities. Tent sites sit under the protection of huge moss-covered maples that tower over an assortment of western Washington foliage—alder, hemlock, salmonberry, salal, and huckleberry. Sword ferns as tall as three feet thrive in the damp, shrouded climes. Madrona trees, with their signature peeling red bark, gnarled limbs, and dark green, all-season leaves, barely cling to the steep and crumbling cliffs above the beach and filter peekaboo saltwater views. Dogwoods dress things up in spring with fresh, white blossoms—a contrast to all that is green, green, green in this classic Northwest setting.

This precious piece of saltwater real estate (heaven knows what staggering price tag it would carry in today's market) was the McLeod family's gift to the state in the late 1940s, when they specified that it be preserved as a park. How lucky we are today that the McLeods were such progressive land stewards!

The campground is set up in loop fashion, with loop A containing most of the tent sites and loop B the domain of those that require hookups (RVs). There are several walk-in sites in loop A as well. The best sites are those outside the loop road because they back up to nothing but thick woods and greenbelt. These sites are farther from the beach, but an easy, well-maintained trail will get you down there in no time. Make sure you're going in the right direction, however. The underbrush is so dense you can't see the water from the campground, and it's easy to get disoriented if you don't have your bearings. When all else fails, follow the signs.

Speaking of beach, Dash Point is one of the few parks south of Seattle that actually has sand to wriggle

RATINGS

Beauty: ✿ ✿ ✿ ✿ ✿
Privacy: ✿ ✿ ✿ ✿
Spaciousness: ✿ ✿ ✿ ✿
Quiet: ✿ ✿ ✿
Security: ✿ ✿ ✿
Cleanliness: ✿ ✿ ✿ ✿

your toes in. Thanks to a 1 percent slope, roughly 2,200 feet extend out into Puget Sound, warming the shallow waters that pass over it and making Dash Point a prized saltwater swimming area. (For the uninformed, Puget Sound temperatures remain a fairly constant 40–50 °F year-round at normal depths, so finding a warm, shallow, sandy spot is a rare treat.) The total saltwater coastline at Dash Point stretches roughly 3,300 feet.

You may want to lay out a summer supper on one of the many (73, count 'em) picnic tables down by the shoreline and let your mind drift back to an earlier time in Puget Sound history. It's 1792 and Captain George Vancouver and his crew have found their way along this uncharted inland body of water. On May 26 the explorers stopped for dinner at Browns Point (the next point south toward Tacoma) and, in the fading twilight, enjoyed the views of the Olympic Mountains and Vashon Island to the west. They would also have enjoyed the light that can linger as late as 11 p.m. in the summertime and were perhaps even treated to one of Puget Sound's showy sunsets. Modern picnickers can admire nearly identical scenes with only the addition of city lights and some urban background noise to remind them that civilization is not far away.

You'll feel the crush of that nearby civilization most oppressively in the summer months, when there will be plenty of it in evidence at Dash Point (traffic is particularly heavy Thursday through Sunday). Overnighters passing through on the I-5 corridor use the park plenty, too. Try to visit during a less crowded time of year—the park is always open. Since it accepts reservations, if you can plan far enough ahead for your summer outing, chances are you'll be assured a site— maybe even the exact one you want.

If you want to balance your wilderness escape with some of what civilization has to offer nearby, both Seattle and Tacoma have their share of activities. The Pike Place Market, the Seattle Center and its landmark Space Needle and flamboyant Experience Music Project, Pioneer Square, waterfront shops and eateries, and the Seattle Art Museum, as well as an interesting collection of neighborhoods ringing the downtown core— all are part of the flavor and excitement of Seattle.

KEY INFORMATION

ADDRESS: Dash Point State Park
5700 Southwest Dash Point Road
Federal Way, WA 98023

INFORMATION: (253) 661-4955

OPEN: All year, with limited winter access

SITES: 114 tent sites

EACH SITE HAS: Picnic table, fire pit with grill, shade trees

ASSIGNMENT: Reservations accepted, call (888) CAMPOUT or (888) 226-7688 (fills up quickly Thursday–Sunday in summer); $7 nonrefundable reservation fee

REGISTRATION: At camp office

FACILITIES: Bathhouse with sinks, flush toilets, showers, and hot water; public telephone; boat put-in; play area; group camp; swimming beach; picnic area; amphitheater

PARKING: At individual sites

FEE: $10 per night primitive site; $16 basic tent camper; $22 full electric hookup

ELEVATION: Sea level

RESTRICTIONS: Pets: On leash
Fires: In fire pits only
Alcohol: Campsites only
Vehicles: RVs and trailers up to 40 feet
Other: 10-day limit on length of stay, May–September 30; 15-day limit, October–April 30

MAP

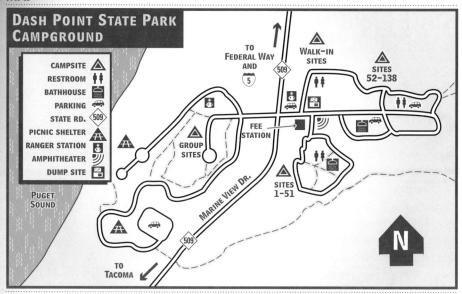

DASH POINT STATE PARK CAMPGROUND

CAMPSITE
RESTROOM
BATHHOUSE
PARKING
STATE RD. 509
PICNIC SHELTER
RANGER STATION
AMPHITHEATER
DUMP SITE

PUGET SOUND

TO FEDERAL WAY AND 5
509
WALK-IN SITES
SITES 52–138
FEE STATION
GROUP SITES
MARINE VIEW DR.
SITES 1–51
509
TO TACOMA

N

GETTING THERE

From Seattle, take the 320th Street exit off I-5 at Federal Way and head west to 21st Avenue SW. Turn right at the T-intersection onto 47th Street SW, and then turn left at the T-intersection of WA 509 (Marine View Drive). The park entrance is about 3 miles south on WA 509. Turn left for the campground. The road to the right takes you down to the day parking area and pathway to the beach.

Tacoma is home to the Washington State Historical Society Museum, the distinctive Tacoma Art Museum, the Chihuly Glass Museum, the Pantages Theater, and Point Defiance Park, Zoo, and Aquarium. You'll find a revitalized urban center, lively old town, and waterfront scenes, with restaurants, taverns, shops, two fishing piers, and a paved promenade along Commencement Bay.

FORT EBEY STATE PARK CAMPGROUND

SITUATED IN blissfully underdeveloped water-front beauty, Fort Ebey is increasingly popular among tent campers and others looking to escape urban life without having to travel too far.

The fort itself was one of four artillery facilities established in 1942 to defend the state during World War II. The other three forts (Casey, Flagler, and Worden) also occupy choice waterfront real estate on either side of Admiralty Inlet, joining Ebey in guarding the mouth of Puget Sound today as historic state parks.

From a tent-camping perspective, Fort Ebey—named for the pioneering Isaac Ebey family that settled the area—is decidedly the least developed. It is evident that every attempt has been made to protect the natural beauty of the place. Old-growth Douglas fir marks this region, which escaped desecration by logging interests. An undergrowth of salal, huckleberry, Scotch broom, and rhododendron has become quite dense over the years, making each campsite decidedly singular and private. In midspring the wild rhododendrons fill the park with a profusion of large, colorful blossoms.

The tenting area is to the left as you pass the campground office; beach access, Lake Pondilla, and picnic areas are to the right. On the way to the campground is the turnoff to the old gun emplacements that have long since been dismantled but continue to instill—even if only momentarily—the sense of vulnerability that prevailed during World War II when one looked out over the wide expanse of the Strait of Juan de Fuca and the Pacific Ocean.

Continuing on to the campground, enter the loop to the right and know that you are passing the best sites early on. If they are empty, grab one. These are pull-throughs but without hookups, so don't feel guilty if your compact car looks a little lost in the parking space. These are the premier bluffside sites with short

> *Hop a ferry boat—preferably the one that leaves from Mukilteo, south of Everett—and head for the western-most tip of Whidbey Island to enjoy one of Washington's newest state parks.*

RATINGS

Beauty: ✪ ✪ ✪ ✪ ✪
Privacy: ✪ ✪ ✪
Spaciousness: ✪ ✪ ✪ ✪
Quiet: ✪ ✪ ✪
Security: ✪ ✪ ✪ ✪ ✪
Cleanliness: ✪ ✪ ✪ ✪

ADDRESS: Fort Ebey State Park 395 North Fort Ebey Road Coupeville, WA 98239

OPERATED BY: Washington State Parks and Recreation Commission

INFORMATION: (360) 678-4636

OPEN: Late February–October 31

SITES: 44 with electricity, 4 utility, 1 group camp for up to 60 people

EACH SITE HAS: Picnic table, fire grill, shade trees

ASSIGNMENT: First come, first served; reservations accepted May 15–September 15, call (888) CAMPOUT or (888) 226-7688

REGISTRATION: At campground office

FACILITIES: Bathhouse with sinks, toilets, showers, hot water; public telephone; boat put-in on lake; picnic area; disabled access; group camp

PARKING: At individual sites

FEE: $16 per night standard, $22 for utility sites

ELEVATION: Sea level

RESTRICTIONS: **Pets:** On leash
Fires: In fire pits only
Alcohol: Permitted
Vehicles: No hookups for RVs or trailers

trail access to the wild, windward side of Whidbey Island. You'll have your own endless view and the sharp taste of the elements if the wind is blowing (chances are good).

This area of western Washington tends to be less rainy than other parts (although every time I've been there, it's been blustery and wet) because it is protected by the "rain shadow" cast by the Olympic Mountains to the west. This said, the weather manages to wreak havoc on the place in other ways. It may be drier at Fort Ebey, but it is not necessarily tamer. The park faces the Strait of Juan de Fuca and is constantly buffeted by Pacific winds.

The delicate composition of glacial debris—sand and gravel—that makes up Whidbey Island is often no match for the howling furies that descend. Point Partridge, which I remember as a high, grassy bluff, has been gnawed and clawed beyond recognition by the vengeance of seasonal storms. More than 2,000 of the majestic old-growth firs that once graced the park grounds toppled like matchsticks in the fierce snow and windstorm of December 1990, and a second storm in the late nineties added insult to injury. Cleanup teams struggled for many years to deal with the downed giants.

There are plenty of activities within the 645-acre park. Beachcombing along the driftwood-laden shoreline. Hiking the wooded trails along the bluffline. Fishing for bass in freshwater Lake Pondilla. Watching a surprising variety of wildlife, including bald eagles, deer, geese, ducks, raccoons, rabbits, pheasant, and grouse. Seeking out the varieties of cactus (yes, cactus!) that grow in this unusual banana belt region of western Washington.

If this doesn't satisfy you, numerous attractions in Coupeville and Oak Harbor may fill in the gaps. There are several other state parks in the neighborhood, too. Of particular note is Fort Casey, which has an interpretive center and is the site of Admiralty Head Lighthouse. Ebeys Landing National Historic Reserve preserves the legacy of the early pioneers.

It is worth noting that the park attendants have been known to turn away as many as 200 cars per day

MAP

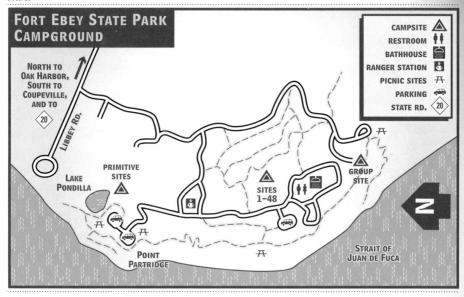

FORT EBEY STATE PARK CAMPGROUND

NORTH TO OAK HARBOR, SOUTH TO COUPEVILLE, AND TO ⟨20⟩

LIBBEY RD.

LAKE PONDILLA

PRIMITIVE SITES

SITES 1-48

GROUP SITE

POINT PARTRIDGE

STRAIT OF JUAN DE FUCA

CAMPSITE	
RESTROOM	
BATHHOUSE	
RANGER STATION	
PICNIC SITES	
PARKING	
STATE RD.	⟨20⟩

N

during heavy summer usage. This Washington State Park takes reservations in the summertime, so either plan far enough ahead or consider the splendor of the off-season (but avoid the hurricane-force winds).

If this is your first time to Fort Ebey State Park, you should know that although signs mark the way to the campground, you will be driving through a light residential area. It may not seem that there is a park nearby, but keep going.

GETTING THERE

From Seattle, drive north on I-5 and WA 526/525 to Mukilteo and the Washington State Ferry terminal for Whidbey Island. Once on the island, follow WA 525 north, pick up WA 20 at Keystone, and continue north to Libbey Road and signs to the park. Total driving distance on the Island is about 35 miles.

Alternate route: From I-5 at Burlington, take WA 20 west and drive down the northern half of Whidbey Island through Deception Pass. Look for Libbey Road and the park turnoff to the right, about 8 miles south of Oak Harbor, not long after Penn Cove.

ILLAHEE STATE PARK CAMPGROUND

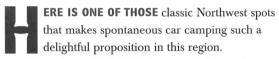

> *Undiscovered yet conve-nient, this lovely place is for those who don't feel like an endless drive to get away from it all.*

RATINGS

Beauty: ✪ ✪ ✪ ✪ ✪
Privacy: ✪ ✪ ✪ ✪
Spaciousness: ✪ ✪ ✪ ✪
Quiet: ✪ ✪ ✪ ✪
Security: ✪ ✪ ✪ ✪
Cleanliness: ✪ ✪ ✪ ✪ ✪

HERE IS ONE OF THOSE classic Northwest spots that makes spontaneous car camping such a delightful proposition in this region.

Situated on a high bluff that guards the southern entrance to Port Orchard Passage, Illahee State Park is a gem of a destination roughly an hour west of Seattle by ferry and about half that amount of time by car from Tacoma. Or you can get there on the Edmonds–Kingston run (just north of Seattle) and sightsee your way south with numerous interesting side trips. With 1,785 feet of saltwater frontage on the bay and a 354-foot dock with a flotilla of moorage buoys, you could easily slip into this quiet haven by boat.

The park faces northeast, out of the way on the northern outskirts of Bremerton and overlooking the west side of Bainbridge Island. Until it was acknowl-edged in a national magazine as a top ten most livable city, Bremerton was known to the outside world mostly as a ship-building port and home to the navy's Pacific fleet. Since then, it hasn't exactly attracted the rich and famous, but when Seattle's housing market went through the roof a few years back and freeway traffic jams reached road-rage proportions, West Sound communities started heavily promoting their affordable housing, stress-free ferry riding, and general quality of life.

Illahe (a Native American word meaning "earth" or "country") is prime real estate supporting the lifestyle to which West Sounders subscribe. It still appears to be unknown to most out-of-towners (too busy searching for their own affordable "illahee," I guess), which is good news for the rest of us. Amid towering and densely clus-tered maples, cedars, Douglas fir, madrona, dogwood, and rhododendron, each campsite is picturesquely and privately shrouded in ferns, salal, huckleberry, black-berry (watch out for the thorns), and salmonberry.

William Bremer, for whom Bremerton is named, first settled in the area around 1888, salivating at the abundant timber resources. Fortunately, he set to work clearing other areas first, and Illahee was spared the ax and chainsaw. The state acquired the park in seven separate parcels, beginning in 1934; much of the original foliage has been left intact. In fact, Illahee is the home of the only remaining stand of old-growth forest in Kitsap County and one of the largest yew trees in the country. This alone makes a visit worth the trip.

After setting up camp and with the sound of sea gulls screeching overhead, take one of the park trails that leads down to the waterfront. The drop is steep, so you'll get a good start on your exercise program. There is a paved roadway down to the water as well, but I advise the path if you intend to walk. The road is sharply inclined and narrow with no room for pedestrians. There's nowhere to go if you happen to meet up with an SUV/boat trailer combination on any of the several blind, hairpin turns along the way.

Park developers got a little carried away with the size of the parking lot down on the beach, but in all likelihood the lot was intended to accommodate the many boaters using the boat launch on busy summer weekends. It's a prime spot to put in and explore the shorelines along the numerous bays, inlets, and passages of Puget Sound. Sea kayaking from this spot is an excellent idea because you can explore the myriad coves, inlets, bays, hooks, points, and passages that define the land.

There's plenty of marine life and the usual assortment of camp critters on shore (squirrels, chipmunks, and raccoons) to observe. At low tide, clamming can be quite good. Crabbing and oystering are options, but check that there are no restrictions first. Red tide and pollution indiscriminately plague beaches around Puget Sound. Generally, there will be signs warning of any current hazards.

The park honors more than just old-growth trees. A veteran's war memorial pays tribute to local fallen heroes, which may help explain the giant gun that sits guarding the entrance to the park (not your typical welcoming attraction at a campground). Other points of interest in the surrounding areas include quaint

KEY INFORMATION

ADDRESS:	Illahee State Park 3540 Bahia Vista Bremerton, WA 98310
OPERATED BY:	Washington State Parks and Recreation Commission
INFORMATION:	(360) 902-8500 or (360) 478-6460
OPEN:	All year
SITES:	25 standard
EACH SITE HAS:	Fire grill, picnic table, water, shade trees
ASSIGNMENT:	First come, first served; no reservations
REGISTRATION:	Self-registration on site
FACILITIES:	Restrooms with toilets, sinks, hot showers; boat launch, mooring buoys, boat dock; public telephone; trailer dump station; horseshoe pits, ball field, playground; group picnic areas with covered kitchens; disabled access
PARKING:	At individual sites and in parking lot at shoreline
FEE:	$15 standard; $10 each additional vehicle
ELEVATION:	500 feet
RESTRICTIONS:	**Pets:** On leash **Fires:** In fire pit **Alcohol:** Only in designated areas **Vehicles:** RVs up to 40 feet; no hookups

MAP

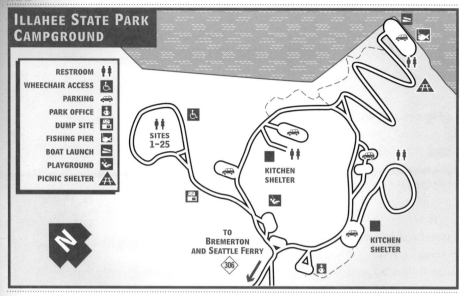

ILLAHEE STATE PARK CAMPGROUND

RESTROOM
WHEECHAIR ACCESS
PARKING
PARK OFFICE
DUMP SITE
FISHING PIER
BOAT LAUNCH
PLAYGROUND
PICNIC SHELTER

SITES 1-25

KITCHEN SHELTER

KITCHEN SHELTER

TO BREMERTON AND SEATTLE FERRY

306

N

GETTING THERE

From the Bremerton ferry terminal, follow WA 303 north (Warren Avenue) to WA 306 (Sylvan Way). Turn right and follow the signs to Illahee. The total distance is about 3 miles.

From Tacoma, cross the Tacoma Narrows Bridge on WA 16 and follow the road about 25 miles to Bremerton. Take the City Center exit (WA 304), which zigzags through town. Keep making the obvious zigzags until you reach WA 303 (Warren Avenue). Turn left and follow the directions above.

Scandinavian Poulsbo, the town of Suquamish and the Suquamish Museum, Port Orchard's antiques malls, the Trident Submarine Warfare Base in Bangor, and the Hood Canal Brewery near Kingston. A number of first-class golf courses are within a short drive of the campground.

LARRABEE STATE PARK CAMPGROUND

CAMPING WITHIN **7** MILES of an urban center doesn't qualify as a true wilderness escape. But when time, inclination, or myriad other factors don't allow you to throw yourself into a far-flung adventure, the unspoiled pleasure of Larrabee State Park can be quite a decent substitute.

Located on 2,683 acres along saltwater Samish Bay south of Bellingham, Larrabee is the oldest state park in Washington. Its designation in 1915 was a mere 20 acres. But with other acquisitions and contributions over the years, the park has been able to protect such a lush growth of Northwest foliage—Douglas fir, western red cedar, hemlock, bigleaf maple, willows, rhododendron, and sword fern—that it is difficult not to think you have ventured miles into a remote and primeval place.

In reality, the way to Larrabee is along one of the most heavily traveled scenic drives in western Washington and perhaps the entire state. Chuckanut Drive is officially known as WA 11 and connects south Bellingham with the farming communities of the Skagit River flats along 25 miles of roadway with numerous stretches that cling precariously to the side of Chuckanut Mountain. A series of wheel-gripping twists and turns eventually gives way to a straightaway that makes you accelerate just for the sheer joy of seeing broad, flat ground all around you.

Chuckanut Drive is famous not only for its suicide turns but also for the stupendous views across Puget Sound to the San Juan archipelago. Scenic overlook turnouts allow you to pause and take a more leisurely gape, not to mention get that string of Mario Andretti wannabes off your tail. A couple of first-rate seafood restaurants along Chuckanut also make the drive a popular outing, but if you are too busy watching the brake lights of the car in front of you, you might miss them the first time through.

> *Only 7 miles from Bellingham, this park will give you a respectable nature fix when you're on a tight schedule.*

RATINGS

Beauty: ✿ ✿ ✿ ✿ ✿
Privacy: ✿ ✿ ✿ ✿
Spaciousness: ✿ ✿ ✿ ✿
Quiet: ✿ ✿ ✿
Security: ✿ ✿ ✿
Cleanliness: ✿ ✿ ✿ ✿ ✿

KEY INFORMATION

ADDRESS: Larrabee State Park
245 Chuckanut Drive
Bellingham, WA
98226

OPERATED BY: Washington State
Parks and Recreation Commission

INFORMATION: (360) 676-2093

OPEN: All year

SITES: 51 standard tent
sites, 26 utility sites,
8 primitive sites

EACH SITE HAS: Picnic table, fire pit
with grill, shade
trees

ASSIGNMENT: First come, first
served; reservations
accepted May 15–
September 15, call
(888) CAMPOUT or
(888) 226-7688; $7
nonrefundable
reservation fee

REGISTRATION: Self-registration on
site

FACILITIES: Bathhouse with
sinks, toilets, showers, hot water; firewood; boat launch
nearby

PARKING: At individual site

FEE: $16 per night; $22
full hookup, $10
primitive; $10 second vehicle

ELEVATION: Sea level

RESTRICTIONS: Pets: On leash
Fires: In fire pits
only
Alcohol: Permitted
in designated sites
Vehicles: RVs to 60
feet (limited availability)

For reasons that defy explanation, Chuckanut Drive attracts a sizable number of cyclists. I don't recommend it myself simply because it is too dangerous. The road is very narrow with minimal shoulders, blind corners, and too many lurching RVs and impatient SUVs for my taste. Aside from an occasional turnout, there is no place to go to avoid or be avoided, short of slamming into the crumbling rock of Chuckanut Mountain or careening over a guardrail into space. The "bike route" marker should have some fine print on it.

So leave the bicycle at home on this trip. You have plenty of hiking trails, pebbled beaches, and rocky tidepools to explore instead. Sea kayaking is also an option, with numerous coves, bays, points, rocks, and islets within easy paddling range. For boaters or saltwater fishing types, there's a boat launch nearby. For freshwater anglers, both Fragrance Lake and Lost Lake are stocked, but they require a little effort to get to (along a 2-mile trail). Bird-watching, swimming, and scuba diving have their seasonal appeal.

If you simply want fresh air and a look at the lay of the land, take a drive up Cleator Road to 1,900-foot Cyrus Gates Overlook for the best possible view of the San Juans. For views of Mount Baker (Washington's third-highest volcano peak, only 30 miles east) and the North Cascade Range, take the short hike to the East Overlook.

Weatherwise, this is coastal Washington, so let's be realistic. Westerly winds carry moisture and cool temperatures most of the year, with late summer and early fall the most dependable times for dry tenting. Even on the hottest summer days, marine breezes chill the skin, and it is a rare evening that doesn't warrant a fleece layer. Summer evenings this close to the Canadian border last a long time; it's not uncommon for the last strains of a fabulous sunset to be visible after 11 p.m.

You'll find the campground to the right as you descend the camp road off Chuckanut Drive. Two small loops flank the entrance to the camping area and feature individual and multiple standard sites. Two larger loops offer standard individual and multiple sites on their perimeter, with the utility sites smartly clustered within. Sites 1 through 29 are close to Chuckanut

MAP

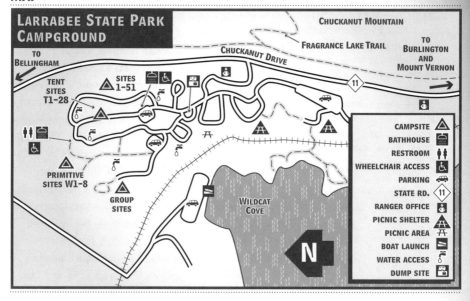

LARRABEE STATE PARK CAMPGROUND

CHUCKANUT MOUNTAIN

FRAGRANCE LAKE TRAIL

TO BURLINGTON AND MOUNT VERNON

CHUCKANUT DRIVE

TO BELLINGHAM

TENT SITES T1-28

SITES 1-51

11

PRIMITIVE SITES W1-8

GROUP SITES

WILDCAT COVE

N

CAMPSITE	▲
BATHHOUSE	🚿
RESTROOM	🚻
WHEELCHAIR ACCESS	♿
PARKING	🚗
STATE RD.	11
RANGER OFFICE	🏠
PICNIC SHELTER	⛺
PICNIC AREA	⊥
BOAT LAUNCH	⊿
WATER ACCESS	🚰
DUMP SITE	🗑

Drive (above you), so, if possible, try for sites 34 through 41. Sites 42 through 46 are tucked among bushy thickets and seemingly private, but keep in mind that the Burlington–Northern Railroad track is just south, and numerous trains (including Amtrak) rumble by day and night. The walk-in sites are probably the best option for both privacy and quiet, but they are not reservable and can easily fill on any given summer weekend. If you can plan ahead for one of the standard sites, do. Reservations should be made as far in advance as possible.

GETTING THERE

Drive north on I-5 to Bellingham and take the turnoff for Chuckanut Drive and Fairhaven. Follow the signs to WA 11 and head south. The entrance to the park is about 7 miles on the right.

LOPEZ FARM COTTAGES AND TENT CAMPING

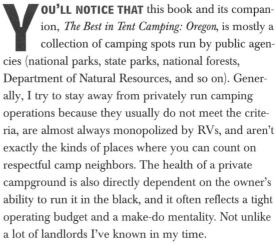

> *This is camping for adults in an indulgent and thoughtfully designed and managed private preserve.*

YOU'LL NOTICE THAT this book and its companion, *The Best in Tent Camping: Oregon,* is mostly a collection of camping spots run by public agencies (national parks, state parks, national forests, Department of Natural Resources, and so on). Generally, I try to stay away from privately run camping operations because they usually do not meet the criteria, are almost always monopolized by RVs, and aren't exactly the kinds of places where you can count on respectful camp neighbors. The health of a private campground is also directly dependent on the owner's ability to run it in the black, and it often reflects a tight operating budget and a make-do mentality. Not unlike a lot of landlords I've known in my time.

Every once in a while, along comes an exception to the rule. Lopez Farm Cottages and Tent Camping easily qualifies as a worthwhile destination for creatively blending this island's most-needed services (thoughtful tent camping and private cottages) tastefully and practically. If you plan to bring the kids, however, think again. Lopez Farm accommodates no one under 14 (except for an adorable assortment of the four-legged variety—mostly lambs, fawns, and baby rabbits).

Just minutes from the Lopez Island Ferry Terminal and only 1 mile from the village of Lopez, Lopez Farm is picturesque—situated in the middle of a broad, rolling meadow defined on three sides by the Lopez Island road system and on one side by forests. Now you might be inclined to protest that a campground bearing the description "bounded on three sides by roadway" can't possibly offer pastoral quiet, but the compound is laid out so expertly that this is a minor consideration.

And if you know anything about the roads on Lopez (besides that everyone waves), then you know that they are busiest when ferries are arriving and

RATINGS

Beauty: ✪ ✪ ✪ ✪
Privacy: ✪ ✪ ✪ ✪ ✪
Spaciousness: ✪ ✪ ✪ ✪ ✪
Quiet: ✪ ✪ ✪
Security: ✪ ✪ ✪ ✪ ✪
Cleanliness: ✪ ✪ ✪ ✪ ✪

departing, which is only a temporary intrusion—and not a very late one at that! Ferries between the mainland ferry terminal at Anacortes, Lopez (the first stop), and the rest of the islands don't offer service much after 9 p.m. on weekdays (about an hour or so later on Friday and Saturday). It's important to know the ferry schedule intimately when traveling in the San Juan Islands, by the way.

The main campground will be on your left as you drive in from Fisherman Bay Road. Follow the road as it curls around to the right, however. At the fork, stay right for campsites 1 through 10; bear left for sites A, B, and C (new in 2004). Find your designated parking area, sign in at the check-in building, and pick up a handy wagon for transporting your camp gear. Since campsites are available on a first-come, first-serve basis (if you haven't reserved your first night in advance by credit card), you'll want to take a look at the sites before you choose. Sites A, B, and C are used as group sites and are available individually if sites 1 through 10 are taken.

Some of the sites in the main camping area have the advantage of being closer to the camp building's amenities, whereas those at the far end of the loop offer maximum privacy. Each has its own "personality" and all come with effects that will remind you of your backyard—hammock, Adirondack chairs, and a table. If I had to pick the optimum spot for my tastes, I would have to say it's site 9, which mixes all the characteristics that will spoil you for camping at Lopez Farm (an easy stroll to the Scandinavian-style camp building, views of sheep resting among the old apple trees, and maybe just a tad more isolation, thanks to a dense cluster of foliage). Hard to beat the bucolic ambience of a Lopez Farm tent-camping experience.

Central to the experience is the camp building—a cleverly designed multiuse facility with lots of natural wood; a giant, covered stone fireplace at one end; and party-sized shower and bathrooms at the other. There are picnic tables both inside and out, barbecues beside the camp building, and even a microwave. Morning coffee (how much more civilized can you get?) will be waiting for you on the pasture side of the camp build-

KEY INFORMATION

ADDRESS: Lopez Farm Cottages and Tent Camping Fisherman Bay Road Lopez, WA 98261

OPERATED BY: John and Ann Warsen, proprietors

INFORMATION: (800) 440-3556; www.lopezfarm cottages.com

OPEN: May–October

SITES: 13 tent sites

EACH SITE HAS: Level tent area, hammock, 2 Adirondack chairs, small table

ASSIGNMENT: First come, first served; reservations can be made in advance with first night's payment via credit card

REGISTRATION: Self check-in

FACILITIES: Wooded setting; camp building with private bathrooms and open-air showers; picnic tables, barbecues; badminton net; complimentary morning coffee; wagons for moving camping equipment

PARKING: In separate area near check-in building

FEE: $33 per site, double occupancy

ELEVATION: Just above sea level

RESTRICTIONS: Pets: No dogs
Fires: Open fires at campsites prohibited; hibachis and cookstoves permitted
Alcohol: Permitted in campsite
Vehicles: No RVs
Other: No children under 14

MAP

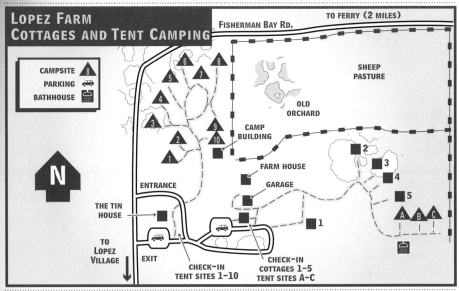

LOPEZ FARM COTTAGES AND TENT CAMPING

FISHERMAN BAY RD.

TO FERRY (2 MILES)

CAMPSITE △8
PARKING 🚐
BATHHOUSE 🚿

SHEEP PASTURE

OLD ORCHARD

CAMP BUILDING

N

FARM HOUSE

GARAGE

THE TIN HOUSE

ENTRANCE

TO LOPEZ VILLAGE

EXIT

CHECK-IN TENT SITES 1-10

CHECK-IN COTTAGES 1-5 TENT SITES A-C

GETTING THERE

From the ferry terminal at Lopez Island in the San Juans, drive 2.6 miles inland towards Lopez Village. The driveway and well-placed sign will be on your left. The entrance is the first driveway you come to; the exit is the second. Follow the signs to either the "Camping" check-in building for sites 1–10, or the "Cottage" check-in building for sites A, B, and C.

ing. Since open fires are not allowed at the campsites, the fireplace will be the main attraction at night. In a storm, it's easy to imagine the roaring blaze kicking off an unplanned get-acquainted session among fellow campers. Maybe even the spark of a romance.

The campground is open only from May to October, but if you find yourself in Lopez in the off-season, Lopez Farm has five comfortably appointed cottages available by reservation all year long. Whether it's camping or cottaging, a visit to Lopez Farm is a definite dose of indulgence. And you're worth it!

SPENCER SPIT STATE PARK CAMPGROUND

A BOOK ABOUT CAR CAMPING in the Northwest would not be complete without at least one listing from the beautiful San Juan Islands archipelago. Selecting one is relatively easy, actually, despite the fact that the San Juan Islands unofficially include 768 exposed rocks, reefs, and islands.

For starters, only 175 of these land formations have been named, and 85 are inaccessible to the public, protected by their designation as the San Juan Islands National Wildlife Refuge. Only five can be reached by ferry either from Anacortes, Washington, on the U.S. side or Sidney, British Columbia, on the Canadian side. Of these, only four maintained campgrounds are accessible by car, one of which is Spencer Spit State Park on Lopez Island. There are many boat-in only campgrounds throughout the islands.

Far from the seasonal rat race and the city-like atmosphere of the much larger but filled-to-overflowing facilities on Orcas and San Juan Islands, Spencer Spit is an excellent base camp for enjoying Lopez and its sister islands by car, foot, or bicycle. The only drawback to lovely little Spencer Spit is the same drawback that plagues all the other islands that are served by the same mode of transit—the Washington State ferry system.

First, plan on becoming a veritable scholar of the ferry schedule. Pick one up when you pay at the toll-booth. Make sure you know that where you want to go is also where the ferry is planning to go. Ditto on when. In the summertime, additional ferries are put on high-volume routes to accommodate the heavy onslaught of tourists and vacationers. This does not mean that all ferries stop at all islands all the time, however. Some ferries stop at some of the islands some of the time. Lopez is one of those "some of the time" islands.

One of the most appealing aspects of Spencer Spit State Park is that you can camp right on the beach—in

> *If you want to see the beautiful San Juan Islands archipelago, this is the place to stay. You can camp right on the beach.*

RATINGS

Beauty: ☆ ☆ ☆ ☆ ☆
Privacy: ☆ ☆ ☆ ☆
Spaciousness: ☆ ☆ ☆ ☆
Quiet: ☆ ☆ ☆ ☆ ☆
Security: ☆ ☆ ☆
Cleanliness: ☆ ☆ ☆ ☆

ADDRESS:	Spencer Spit State Park RR 2, Box 3600 Lopez, WA 98261
OPERATED BY:	Washington State Parks and Recreation Commission
INFORMATION:	(360) 468-2251
OPEN:	March–October
SITES:	37 standard; 15 primitive
EACH SITE HAS:	Fire grill, picnic table
ASSIGNMENT:	First come, first served; reservations accepted May 15–September 15; call (888) CAMPOUT or (888) 226-7688
REGISTRATION:	Self-registration on site
FACILITIES:	Bathhouse with sinks, toilets, no showers; dump station; 2 group camps with a variety of camping options for small or large groups
PARKING:	In campground and at some individual sites; parking for beach sites near trailhead
FEE:	$15 standard sites; $10 primitive sites
ELEVATION:	Sea level
RESTRICTIONS:	**Pets:** On leash **Fires:** In fire pits **Alcohol:** Permitted **Vehicles:** Self-contained RVs up to 28 feet; no hookups

designated areas, of course. You will have to pack your gear down from the parking lot above. With the park's reputation for excellent crabbing and clamming, it's worth considering making some of that gear the items you'll need to catch your dinner—a bucket or two, sand shovel, crab net, bait, cookpot. Maybe it seems a bit cumbersome, but the rewards will make the effort a distant memory.

Lopez Island is, in my estimation, the premier bicycling island of the San Juans and can easily be covered in a day of riding if you're accustomed to 40 miles or so. Except for the hill up from the ferry terminal, which you will most likely ascend by car anyway, Lopez features mildly rolling farmland with paved roads and a noticeable lack of traffic—even on weekends. It's possible that you'll encounter more bicycles than cars on any given day during the summer.

One of my favorite pastimes on Lopez is riding out to Shark Reef Park with the three B's—a book, binoculars, and a brown-bag lunch—to watch the sea lions that sprawl en masse on the offshore rocks. From your vantage point at Shark Reef, you can also look far across the San Juan Channel to windswept Cattle Point on San Juan Island, where the only sand dunes in the entire island group exist.

Other points of interest on Lopez Island include the village of Lopez, which has some excellent restaurants, interesting shops, and a small museum. Richardson and Mackaye Harbor at the island's southern tip are also highly scenic spots easily reached by car or bicycle. The ferry from Lopez takes you directly into Friday Harbor on San Juan Island and Orcas on (what else?) Orcas Island, both thriving business districts. Unless you're interested in touring the other islands extensively, it's fastest and cheapest just to walk onto the ferry from Lopez and kick around Friday Harbor and Orcas on foot.

The climate of the San Juan Islands is practically unique. Although westerly marine winds can bring a change in the weather at any time, the islands fall under the Olympic Mountains' rain shadow that extends northeast across the Strait of Juan de Fuca. As a result, rainfall averages only about 15 to 25 inches

MAP

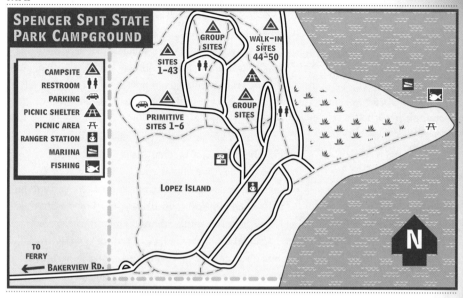

SPENCER SPIT STATE PARK CAMPGROUND

CAMPSITE △
RESTROOM ♛
PARKING 🚐
PICNIC SHELTER ⛺
PICNIC AREA 🛆
RANGER STATION 🚹
MARIINA 🚩
FISHING 🐟

GROUP SITES

WALK-IN SITES 44-50

SITES 1-43

GROUP SITES

PRIMITIVE SITES 1-6

LOPEZ ISLAND

TO FERRY
← BAKERVIEW RD.

N

per year. Summers can be quite hot—some of my deepest tans are from San Juan bicycle trips—and the lovely, balmy days of autumn are unsurpassed. Even in summer, however, nights are chilly enough for a campfire to be appreciated.

GETTING THERE

Take a ferry from the Anacortes terminal to Lopez Island. The ride to Lopez is less than 45 minutes one way. From the ferry terminal at the northern end of Lopez Island, take Ferry Road south, and follow the signs to the park. The total distance from the ferry terminal is barely 5 miles.

NORTHERN **CASCADES**
AND ENVIRONS

FALLS CREEK CAMPGROUND

DON'T TRY TO FIGURE IT OUT. Chewuch. I mean Chewack. No, Chewuck. Or is it Chewuk? Chewak? OK, enough. I don't really know which is correct and, apparently, neither does anyone else in the state. You'll find all varieties on maps and road signs and in reference books and guidebooks. Some maps even use Chewuch and Chewack side by side. There is consistency in the inconsistency at least.

Perhaps the confusion dates back to as early as the mid-1800s when the *Chewuch* River (I'm making an executive decision here) first appeared as such on maps of the region. This area of the Methow Valley was just starting to open up to mining activity about that time, but it's likely that the explorers and traders who preceded this frenzy were responsible for naming the natural features as they went. As with many parts of Washington State, history was not recorded until there was an actual settlement in any given place, so much of what we know about earlier times is gleaned from the journals and diaries of adventurous souls that came seeking their fortunes—or at least an interesting route to them.

The Chewuch River valley has remained relatively undeveloped since its first discovery because it is overshadowed by the more prominent, much-publicized and well-traveled Methow Valley with Western-style Winthrop at its epicenter. Gracing the land throughout is the meandering charm of the crystal-clear Methow River as it makes its way southeast to the Columbia River through rolling rangelands dotted with groves of cottonwood, aspen, tamarack, and pine. Explorers to the Methow (pronounced met' how) Valley these days come in the form of well-fleeced outdoor enthusiasts who have been lured from the wet side of the mountains in their Range Rovers

> *Falls Creek is not far from the bustle of western-style Winthrop but is on a good fishing stream and has a roaring falls nearby.*

RATINGS

Beauty: ✪ ✪ ✪ ✪
Privacy: ✪ ✪ ✪
Spaciousness: ✪ ✪ ✪ ✪ ✪
Quiet: ✪ ✪ ✪ ✪ ✪
Security: ✪ ✪ ✪
Cleanliness: ✪ ✪ ✪ ✪ ✪

ADDRESS: Falls Creek
Campground
c/o Methow Ranger
District
24 West Chewuch
Road
Winthrop, WA 98862

OPERATED BY: Okanogan National
Forest

INFORMATION: (509) 996-4003

OPEN: June–October

SITES: 7

EACH SITE HAS: Picnic table, fire pit
with grill

ASSIGNMENT: First come, first
served

REGISTRATION: On site

FACILITIES: Vault toilets;
garbage service; no
piped water; acces-
sible trail to falls
across road

PARKING: At individual site

FEE: $5

ELEVATION: 2,100 feet

RESTRICTIONS: Pets: On leash
Fires: In fire pits
only
Alcohol: Permitted
Vehicles: RVs and
trailers up to 18 feet
long

and Subarus to the dry, sun-drenched eastern brink of the North Cascades.

Finding the Chewuch River and, ultimately, Falls Creek Campground, is as easy as looking down at it when you drive over the bridge that brings you into Winthrop from the west on WA 20. Turn left at the intersection, try not to pick off a pedestrian from the throngs, battle your way to the end of town, and continue north. Either the Eastside Chewack (oops, Chewuch) River Road or the West take you where you need to go; just follow signs to FS 51. In no time, you will feel the claustrophobic impact of "TMT" (too many tourists) slip away as you beat feet up the narrow Chewuch River canyon to your destination.

Now, I must warn you: the upper Chewuch Valley has been "charred up" very recently with forest fires, and the scene further up FS 51 and FS 5160 to road's end at Thirtymile Campground (what's left of it) is a shocker. This was the site of the tragic Thirtymile Fire that took the lives of Forest Service workers in July 2001 and was also part of a second blaze—the Farewell Fire—that destroyed 81,000 acres in August 2003. A memorial commemorates the four who gave their lives trying to combat the Thirtymile blaze that was started by—it grieves me to say—an uncontrolled cooking fire. Farewell was started by lightning and roared out of control for nearly six weeks, costing $36 million and making it the largest Pacific Northwest fire in the disastrously dry 2003 season.

Fortunately, Falls Creek Campground was just outside the fire line and is the embodiment of the campgrounds that fell victim inside the line. Simple, rustic, and unadorned with man-made amenities—except for a hand pump and vault toilet—it is richly quiet with the sounds of the Chewuch shushing by, the warm summer wind sighing in the pines, birds twittering, and chipmunks chiding. Beds of pine needles make for soft tent pads. Large sites with parking spaces away from the camp area afford privacy, and low-growing shrubbery present a clean, uncluttered profile.

With only seven sites from which to choose (all stretched along the curving bank of the Chewuch), it's splitting hairs to say which one is best. If sites 3, 4, or 5

MAP

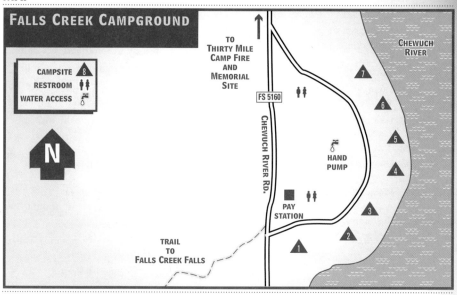

FALLS CREEK CAMPGROUND

CAMPSITE **8**
RESTROOM
WATER ACCESS

N

TO
THIRTY MILE
CAMP FIRE
AND
MEMORIAL
SITE

FS 5160

CHEWUCH RIVER RD.

HAND
PUMP

PAY
STATION

CHEWUCH
RIVER

7

6

5

4

3

2

1

TRAIL
TO
FALLS CREEK FALLS

are available, this puts you closest to the river and away from either end of the camp road where it leaves and returns to FS 51.

Staying at Falls Creeks Campground gives you the daily treat of Falls Creek Falls across the road and up an accessible quarter-mile trail. Nature's open-air shower. After a hot, dusty mountain scramble on foot or bike, the tumult of water falling off the end of Eight-mile Ridge sends delicious spray cascading over you as you approach the grotto.

The Forest Service is currently restoring many of the trails and trailheads that were consumed by fire and were once popular jump-offs into the Pasayten Wilderness in the upper Chewuch, but it will be quite some time before the terrain is user-friendly to my mind. There are better hiking options up FS 37 into the Tiffany Mountain area above the Boulder Creek and North Fork Salmon Creek watersheds. Though not as large a roadless area as the hallowed Pasayten, Tiffany Mountain has been considered for Research Natural Area status because it has unique ecosystems.

In the tradition of a bygone era, explore away!

GETTING THERE

From Winthrop, drive 6.5 miles north on CR 1213 (West Chewuch Road) then continue north 5 miles on FS 51 and 5160 to the campground.

HART'S PASS
CAMPGROUND

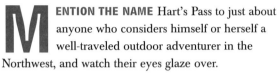

> *Remote and spectacu-larly beautiful, this small tent-only camp-ground is an outdoor adventurer's dream. Get there before the snow!*

MENTION THE NAME Hart's Pass to just about anyone who considers himself or herself a well-traveled outdoor adventurer in the Northwest, and watch their eyes glaze over.

When I first started asking around for camp-ground suggestions in the North Cascades ten years ago, I got as many different suggestions as the number of people I asked. Except that they would always end by saying (almost as an afterthought, so they wouldn't risk offending me), with a cautious sidelong glance, "Of course, you've already got Hart's Pass?" Some-thing between a question and a statement.

For those of you who thought you were somehow going to be able to keep this magical place to yourself, I'm sorry. Ten years after its first appearance as one of the entries in the combined edition, it continues to delight and amaze those discovering it for the first time and the rest of us who won't let go. While the camp-ground itself is tiny and can accommodate only five independent parties, there are plenty of open spaces in the mix of peaks and meadows and forests and trails in just about every direction to lose yourself and get away from the pack. In no time, you'll be rambling the heady altitudes of this prototypical North Cascades terrain in isolated bliss.

What Hart's Pass Campground has going for it in a big way is that you have just driven to the veritable western edge of the massive Pasayten Wilderness, a 505,524-acre roadless tract that extends north to the Canadian border and east to the ridgetops above the Okanogan Valley. Within this territory are 1,000 miles of trails, many of them unmaintained and lead-ing into some of the most difficult terrain in the entire Washington Cascades range. Out of the metamorphic rock, Ice Age glaciers produced an intimidating collection of razor-like ridges, deep valley troughs,

RATINGS

Beauty: ✿ ✿ ✿ ✿ ✿
Privacy: ✿ ✿ ✿
Spaciousness: ✿ ✿ ✿
Quiet: ✿ ✿ ✿ ✿ ✿
Security: ✿ ✿ ✿
Cleanliness: ✿ ✿ ✿ ✿

cirques, and couloirs that tests the most skilled mountaineers.

If you're not quite up to tackling nature at its rugged best, try a simpler approach with a drive up to Slate Peak Lookout. This is the highest point in Washington State that is accessible by car. Once one of 93 manned Forest Service lookouts in the North Cascades range, Slate Peak (at 7,440 feet) offers identification displays of the endless peaks, passes, and ridges visible from its 360-degree viewing area.

Passing near camp, the Pacific Crest National Scenic Trail is the major north–south thoroughfare for foot travel. It can be followed in either direction for those wishing to further sample North Cascades beauty. Wide meadows burst with nearly six dozen flowering varieties of plant life at the height of their bloom (at this altitude and latitude, that tends to be late July to mid-August).

The road into Hart's Pass from Mazama (a tedious 12 miles) is not recommended for extra-wide or low-clearance vehicles. For those of you who are daring enough to continue beyond Hart's Pass by car, there are some points of historical interest to reward your perseverance. I'll warn you now: the road gets even rougher down into the Slate Creek Valley, where evidence of mining activity from the 1880s and 1890s still lingers. Down the road from Chancellor, en route to Barron, is an abandoned building that once served as the stage stop and post office for the mining community before the Hart's Pass road was built. If you can get there, the area around Chancellor and Barron is worth investigation.

A word of caution about traveling to these remote North Cascades destinations: Mazama offers little in the way of services, and there is really nothing substantial between Winthrop to the east on WA 20 and Marblemount to the west—a stretch of 100 spectacularly scenic but civilization-free miles.

Despite its ranking as one of the ten most scenic drives in the United States, North Cascades Highway is not open year-round. It is usually the first of the east–west highways to close for heavy snowfall (normally off-limits November to April). You may want to

KEY INFORMATION

ADDRESS:	Hart's Pass Campground c/o Methow Valley Ranger District 24 West Chewuch Road Winthrop, WA 98862
OPERATED BY:	Okanogan National Forest
INFORMATION:	(509) 996-4003 or (509) 996-4000 (Methow Valley Visitor Center)
OPEN:	Mid-July–late September
SITES:	5
EACH SITE HAS:	Picnic table, fire ring
ASSIGNMENT:	First come, first served; no reservations
REGISTRATION:	Self-registration on site
PARKING:	In campground
FEE:	$5
ELEVATION:	6,198 feet
RESTRICTIONS:	Pets: On leash Fires: In fire pits only Alcohol: Permitted Vehicles: No RVs or trailers Other: No water; pack out garbage

MAP

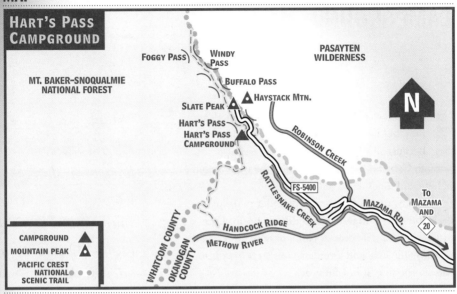

HART'S PASS CAMPGROUND

MT. BAKER-SNOQUALMIE NATIONAL FOREST

FOGGY PASS

WINDY PASS

PASAYTEN WILDERNESS

BUFFALO PASS

SLATE PEAK

HAYSTACK MTN.

HART'S PASS
HART'S PASS CAMPGROUND

ROBINSON CREEK

N

RATTLESNAKE CREEK

FS-5400

MAZAMA RD.

To MAZAMA AND 20

WHATCOM COUNTY
OKANOGAN COUNTY

HANDCOCK RIDGE

METHOW RIVER

CAMPGROUND
MOUNTAIN PEAK
PACIFIC CREST NATIONAL SCENIC TRAIL

GETTING THERE

From Mazama (about 15 miles northwest of Winthrop just off WA 20), follow Mazama Road (Lost Creek Road) about 6 miles to FS 5400. The campground is 12 slow, rough miles up FS 5400.

beat the snow with an early fall camping trip to Hart's Pass just to take in the lovely autumn colors that adorn the length of the highway. If you're thinking of going right after the snowmelt, keep in mind that the mosquitoes and horseflies will be at their worst then.

Travel tip: as of summer 2003, Hart's Pass is the only camping option in the area, and with only five sites—all first come, first served—you may find yourself having to take a number. Meadows Campground, formerly about a mile due south of Hart's Pass on FS 500, had 14 sites but fell victim to a wildfire that came dangerously close to Hart's Pass. If Hart's Pass is full, the closest campgrounds are Ballard and River Bend back down on the Methow River.

What a shame to lose Meadows, but thank heavens that the fickle nature of forest fires saw Hart's Pass spared.

8/2010
Meadows CG has been rebuilt by surrounded by burned trees - star gazing would be the best here.

Meadows very open so lots windy ...

9/22 - 9/25/11 stayed at Meadows CG, Harts Pass 3 nites. Site #12 on end was more private, few other campers on beautiful fall weekend. Last weekend of high hunt so hunters & hikers around, mostly hikers on PCT. Hiked to Silver Lake in F'air & windy, Pass in Sat. Great weather until Sat. night, Sunday. Lots of birds, esp. raptors. Stars were amazing.

HOZOMEEN CAMPGROUND

I HAD BEEN TRYING to get to Hozomeen all summer, but for one reason or another (and largely because of its remoteness and accessibility through Canada), I could never find the right amount of time and itinerary to make it happen.

Finally, on a fall-feeling September morning, I packed the car and just started driving north. I predicted I'd be at Hozomeen easily in time for a picnic lunch by the lake and a rendez-vous with friends for late-afternoon golf in Chilliwack.

Well, here's the word on that idea: Don't try to make Hozomeen anything shorter than a long weekend outing. Just go, take proof of citizenship (as of April 2005, a passport is required in and out of the country), and enjoy! As they say in Canada, it's out there, eh? But well worth the slow, denture-rattling torture of nearly 80 gravel round-trip miles (much of it washboard or sharp rocks or both)—the reward a spectacular lakeside setting in the remote northern reaches of the Ross Lake National Recreation Area.

It seems that topography and history were the driving forces in the creation of Hozomeen, not unlike many backcountry outposts that have their own boom-and-bust stories. Early-day loggers felled as many trees as possible in the Skagit Valley before Ross Dam was built and floated their bounty to the north end of the lake, which was the easiest way out of the steep-walled valley. Using the road that today is the campground access road, they trucked the logs to the Fraser River and sent them downriver to sawmills in Puget Sound. No NAFTA encumbrances in those days—just get the job done. Hozomeen is essentially the base camp from which the logs left the lake for their circuitous journey.

Today the campground stretches along the upper east bank of Ross Lake in obscure simplicity but with plenty of trees still standing. There is a manned ranger

> *It's out there, eh? You have to go through Canada to get here, but your reward is a spectacular setting in the only established public campground on Ross Lake that you can drive to.*

RATINGS

Beauty: ✪ ✪ ✪ ✪ ✪
Privacy: ✪ ✪ ✪ ✪
Spaciousness: ✪ ✪ ✪ ✪ ✪
Quiet: ✪ ✪ ✪ ✪ ✪
Security: ✪ ✪ ✪ ✪ ✪
Cleanliness: ✪ ✪ ✪ ✪ ✪

KEY INFORMATION

ADDRESS: Hozomeen
Campground
c/o Ross Lake
National Recreation
Area
810 WA 20
Sedro–Woolley, WA
98284-1239

OPERATED BY: North Cascades
National Park

INFORMATION: (360) 856-5700, ext.
515

OPEN: May 20–October 31

SITES: 122

EACH SITE HAS: Picnic table, fire pit
with grill

ASSIGNMENT: First come, first
served

REGISTRATION: Not necessary

FACILITIES: Vault toilets; piped
water; boat launch;
ranger station; no
garbage service

PARKING: At individual site

FEE: No fee

ELEVATION: 1,640 feet

RESTRICTIONS: **Pets:** On leash
Fires: In fire pits
only
Alcohol: Permitted
Vehicles: Trailers
and RVs up to 22
feet long
Other: Firewood
gathering prohibited

station during the high season (not surprising, I guess, since this is the only vehicular access into the national recreation area and park). There is good reason to govern the various populaces that arrive because this is indeed a "wilderness" park (with 93 percent of the land so designated) and there are plenty of dos and don'ts to inform the uninitiated. The ranger station also serves as the unofficial border demarcation; the short Trail of the Obelisk through the woods leads to the official one. The original customs cabin sits beside the parking area for the Hozomeen Lake trailhead.

Past the ranger station is the best thing that could have happened at Hozomeen—a separate area for the modern-day Conestoga wagons, appropriately named "Winnebago Flats." Continue past Winnebagoland and you'll find your choice of excellent, spacious campsites set in two loops among dense stands of Douglas fir, western red cedar, and hemlock that provide filtered views of the lake. I recommend the lower loop because it is closer to the lake and away from the hubbub that can characterize the upper loop, which is so close to the Hozomeen Lake trailhead and just up from the boat docks frequented by anglers and the water taxi (more on that in *Getting There*).

Most sites come with a view of the ridgetops across the lake that suggest the glorious surroundings that can best be enjoyed by hitting the trail. Unfortunately, blocked from view by these immediate peaks to the west stands the famous Picket Range, a jumble of glacier and snow-clad granite hulks averaging 8,000 feet high and being almost worshiped by the technical climbing crowd.

On this east side of the lake you need no involved climbing gear to relax beside the deep and pure Hozomeen Lake after hiking a moderate 3.5 miles. Take in the lofty crags of Hozomeen (means "sharp like a knife" in a Native American dialect) Mountain that deserve respect in their own right at 8,066 feet.

In contrast to this picnic outing, the whole hike is the East Bank Trail that runs between Hozomeen and ends at WA 20 just east of Ross Dam at the southern end of the lake. This is 31 miles of ever-changing but endless views from a route that rambles along the

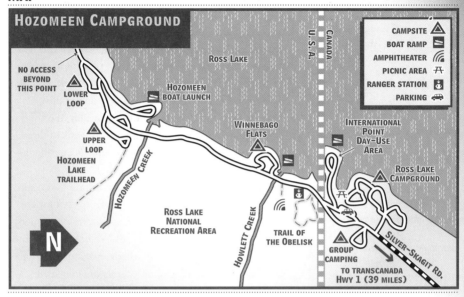

HOZOMEEN CAMPGROUND

NO ACCESS BEYOND THIS POINT

LOWER LOOP

ROSS LAKE

HOZOMEEN BOAT LAUNCH

UPPER LOOP

HOZOMEEN LAKE TRAILHEAD

HOZOMEEN CREEK

WINNEBAGO FLATS

U.S.A. / CANADA

INTERNATIONAL POINT DAY-USE AREA

ROSS LAKE CAMPGROUND

ROSS LAKE NATIONAL RECREATION AREA

HOWLETT CREEK

TRAIL OF THE OBELISK

GROUP CAMPING

SILVER-SKAGIT RD.

TO TRANSCANADA HWY 1 (39 MILES)

CAMPSITE
BOAT RAMP
AMPHITHEATER
PICNIC AREA
RANGER STATION
PARKING

N

shoreline, rises over mini-passes, and winds through peaceful valleys that were once alive with trapping, mining, and prospecting activity. The park service maintains designated campsites along the trail and interpretive plaques at points of interest. Overnight stays along the East Bank Trail and all other backcountry trips require permits (available at Hozomeen).

The other primary activity at Hozomeen is fishing. The best sites will be away from the shoreline, which means you need a boat. Dragging a boat into Hozomeen over a miserable road is not my idea of a quiet escape, but to each his or her own.

Note: If you want to avoid the long drive and nasty road, another option for getting to the campground requires traveling light. For a fee (and with a backcountry permit), you can get delivered to Hozomeen via the water taxi that operates out of Ross Lake Resort on the south end of the lake (accessible via WA 20) east of Newhalem. Call the resort for details at (206) 386-4437.

GETTING THERE

Hozomeen is accessible by automobile only through Canada. Go east from Abbotsford, British Columbia, on TransCanada Highway 1 to the town of Hope. Turn south on Silver–Skagit Road, following signs to Skagit Provincial Park, Ross Lake Campground, and International Point (on the British Columbia side). Continue south, and after 38 miles of rough, gravel road and a backup-free border crossing, you'll enter the Hozomeen complex.

MINERAL PARK CAMPGROUND

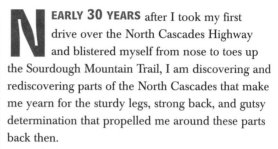

> *This "secret" backdoor access that everyone knows about is a great base camp for exploring the wonders of the North Cascades National Park.*

NEARLY **30 YEARS** after I took my first drive over the North Cascades Highway and blistered myself from nose to toes up the Sourdough Mountain Trail, I am discovering and rediscovering parts of the North Cascades that make me yearn for the sturdy legs, strong back, and gutsy determination that propelled me around these parts back then.

I think it took me this long to make my way to Mineral Park because in the height of my backcountry-tripping days, the phrases "Cascade Pass" and "absurdly crowded" were almost always mentioned in the same sentence. I never had any interest in the Cascade River Road because it provided the easiest access to the most popular trail in the entire North Cascades National Park and associated recreation areas—the last place I wanted to be. I know some of you are shaking your heads in disbelief at this admission and what I've been missing. I know because I'm doing it, too.

At any rate, I have finally ventured up the Cascade River Road twice now in the past year, and let me tell you, thank heaven for places like Mineral Park! Being a born-again car camper, I'm content to know that I'll be just getting back from my invigorating day hike to Cascade Pass and Sahale Arm (weekday only, as this remains an absurdly crowded weekend outing) and settling in for a quiet evening beside the swift-flowing Cascade River while the backpacking crowd fights over the few overloved high-country spots.

Located just outside the western boundary of the North Cascades National Park South Unit, Mineral Park came as close as any campground can to being wiped out in the fall floods of 2003. This stretch of the Cascade River was particularly hard hit, and the devastation was still quite evident in the early summer of 2004. Where campsites and parking spurs

RATINGS

Beauty: ✿ ✿ ✿ ✿ ✿
Privacy: ✿ ✿ ✿ ✿
Spaciousness: ✿ ✿ ✿ ✿
Quiet: ✿ ✿ ✿ ✿
Security: ✿ ✿ ✿
Cleanliness: ✿ ✿ ✿ ✿ ✿

had previously existed, huge sections of bank disintegrated into the river. The center of the river now sports massive islands of debris that look as though some very large, overzealous beavers went berserk. Much work has been done to repair the damage on land, including erecting steely new bridges to replace those that were probably pulverized into toothpicks and spit out downriver.

The good news is that the Cascade River Road, closed because of the flooding just beyond Mineral Park, reopened late in summer 2004. Although you missed the opportunity to enjoy Mineral Park in its temporary road's-end solitude, we must give a hearty thanks to all the dedicated road and trail crews who had a hand in restoring this vital avenue and access to the alpine splendors above.

Mineral Park is actually two campgrounds split by the North Fork of the Cascade River as it merges with the South Fork to create the main Cascade River right in front of your eyes. The western area has more sites that are closer to the river, are more generously spaced, and have more of an open feel. The eastern area is a mix of individual and multiple sites lying beneath a shadowy canopy of evergreens, a picnic area, several sites with a common parking area, and a lone site (8) in a pleasant little private glade on the shoulder of the North Fork.

Surprisingly for a campground with few amenities (garbage cans but no piped water), it is possible to reserve certain sites through the National Recreation Reservation System (see *Key Information*). Perhaps because Mineral Park is a national park access point, the Forest Service decided to offer reservations for a number of sites.

The terrain here is steep, vertical hikes being the primary activity. Aside from the Cascade Pass Trail (which links with other routes within the North Cascades National Park network), there are less strenuous and involved choices for day hikes outside the park's domain, namely at Hidden Lakes and Monogram Lake (both accessed by the Cascade River Road heading toward Marblemount). Chances are that there will be fewer people on these trails any day of the week.

KEY INFORMATION

ADDRESS:	Mineral Park c/o Mt. Baker Ranger District 810 WA 20 Sedro-Woolley, WA 98284
OPERATED BY:	Mount Baker–Snoqualmie National Forest
INFORMATION:	(360) 856-5700; (877) 444-6777; www.reserveusa.com
OPEN:	Memorial Day weekend through Labor Day weekend
SITES:	22 (8 east, 14 west)
EACH SITE HAS:	Picnic table, fire pit with grill
ASSIGNMENT:	Reservation and nonreservation sites
REGISTRATION:	On site
FACILITIES:	Vault toilets; garbage service; no piped water
PARKING:	At individual site
FEE:	$11
ELEVATION:	1,650 feet
RESTRICTIONS:	**Pets:** On leash **Fires:** In fire pits only **Alcohol:** Permitted **Vehicles:** Not recommended

MAP

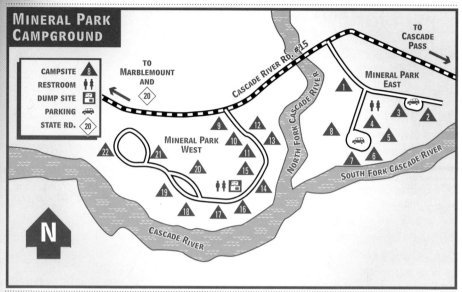

MINERAL PARK CAMPGROUND

CAMPSITE
RESTROOM
DUMP SITE
PARKING
STATE RD.

TO MARBLEMOUNT AND

TO CASCADE PASS

CASCADE RIVER RD. #15

MINERAL PARK EAST

MINERAL PARK WEST

NORTH FORK CASCADE RIVER

SOUTH FORK CASCADE RIVER

CASCADE RIVER

N

GETTING THERE

From Marblemount, pick up Cascade River Road at the intersection where WA 20 takes a 90-degree bend to the east and the Cascade Road immediately crosses the Skagit River. Drive 15 miles on paved, then gravel, road to the campground.

Fishing was probably decent at Mineral Park in the preflood era, but with the flow of the river altered dramatically by countless snags, it would be better attempted closer to the Skagit where it widens and the water/debris ratio favors the H_2O.

For all intents and purposes, Mineral Park is a tent-camping delight even if you do nothing but sit by the river with a good book in hand. For armchair alpinists such as myself, I heartily recommend *North Cascades Crest: Notes and Images from America's Alps* by James Martin. Much of his discourse and photography record and reflect the glaciated heights just above and behind you.

PANORAMA POINT
CAMPGROUND

MANY PURIST Northwest wilderness-goers purposefully overlook camping options at places like Baker Lake simply because they don't feel that they're truly getting a pristine experience if they can hear machines.

In the case of Panorama Point Campground midway up the western shore, that sound will most likely be the gentle buzz of small outboard motors as fishermen putt-putt around in search of the best spots to hook their daily catch. They have their choice of such delights as rainbow, cutthroat, or Dolly Varden trout; kokanee salmon; and whitefish.

This is, indeed, a fisherman's lake. But with miles and miles of Forest Service roads and trails that take you to soothing hot springs and deep into two designated wildernesses, a national recreation area, a national park, and an undeveloped eastern lakeshore, one can hardly complain that there's no getting away from things here. Just make sure you have a good Forest Service map and trail guides of the area before you find yourself at the mercy of the purists.

To the west of Panorama Point lies the glacier-encrusted mass of Mount Baker. This is Washington State's third-highest volcano and is active only thermally as far as geologists can determine. Designated wilderness surrounds Mount Baker and is adjacent to national recreation areas on both north and south flanks of the mountain. Here you'll find unlimited hiking, backpacking, skiing, and climbing opportunities, depending on which season you choose to travel.

It's best to check with the agencies that oversee these areas for special conditions and restrictions. Backpackers, for instance, will need permits for overnight trips into the backcountry.

North of the campground is the equally spectacular Mount Shuksan, a craggy sentinel of snow, ice, and rock

> *This is a fisherman's lake, but there's lots for others to do, too.*

RATINGS

Beauty: ✿ ✿ ✿ ✿ ✿
Privacy: ✿ ✿ ✿ ✿
Spaciousness: ✿ ✿ ✿ ✿
Quiet: ✿ ✿ ✿
Security: ✿ ✿ ✿ ✿
Cleanliness: ✿ ✿ ✿ ✿ ✿

ADDRESS: Panorama Point
Campground
c/o Mount Baker
Ranger District
2105 WA 20
Sedro-Woolley, WA
98284

OPERATED BY: Mount Baker–
Snoqualmie
National Forest;
Conservation
Resources provides
concession service in
summer

INFORMATION: (360) 856-5700

OPEN: May–mid-September

SITES: 16

EACH SITE HAS: Picnic table, fire pit
with grill, shade
trees

ASSIGNMENT: First come, first
served; reservations
accepted for 9 sites,
call Northwest
Recreation Reserva-
tion Service, (877)
444-6777; www.
reserveusa.com.

REGISTRATION: Self-registration on
site

FACILITIES: Vault toilets; firewood; store, café,
and ice within 1
mile; boat ramp
nearby

PARKING: At individual sites

FEE: $15 per night

ELEVATION: 800 feet

RESTRICTIONS: **Pets:** On leash
Fires: In fire pit only
Alcohol: Permitted
Vehicles: RVs and
trailers up to 21 feet
Other: Permits for
overnight backpack-
ing; parking permit
to park at trailhead;
reservations require
3-day minimum stay

that is the gateway for foot travelers approaching North Cascades National Park from the west. There could be no more fitting prototype to the challenging terrain than that embodied in names like Mount Despair, Damnation Park, Mount Challenger, Mount Terror, Mount Fury, and Jagged Ridge. These are but a few of the numerous natural shrines in the northern sector of North Cascades National Park that have been immortalized in the minds and journals of many a mountaineer.

East across Baker Lake is the smallest of the eight wilderness areas in the Mount Baker–Snoqualmie National Forest. Despite its diminutive size (14,300 acres), the Noisy–Diobsud Wilderness is a place to be reckoned with. Elevations range from 2,000 to 6,234 feet, with only 2 miles of maintained trails. It is, for all intents and purposes, a place for experienced climbers and scramblers who are looking for their own personal meccas.

The entire expanse of national forest and parklands around Panorama Point can be quite wet and chilly. Although the campground is only 800 feet in elevation, conditions are more representative of those higher up because the lake captures moisture-laden clouds that drift into its basin. Rainfall averages 40 inches in the lowlands, with up to 100 inches of snow recorded regularly at the highest points.

Lush vegetation is the result of all this moisture and much of the land remains this way due to the extreme contours that have prevented loggers from getting at the plentiful bounty. Where loggers can't go, however, bugs can. A spruce beetle infestation set in a few years ago, and the forest is noticeably affected with browned, dreary limbs on the Engelmann Spruce stands as you drive up the Baker Lake Road. Forest fires and selective thinning will eventually clear up the problem, but in the meantime, look forward to the views out over the lake from your campsite.

I revisited Panorama Point the summer after the floods of 2003 and found that it had fared rather well, considering the dire news reports and glum forecasts from the Forest Service. I wasn't there for the clean up in the spring, however, so I can only assume that certain miracles were performed. Many thanks to the

MAP

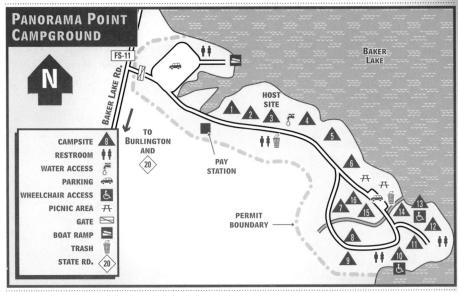

PANORAMA POINT CAMPGROUND

FS-11

BAKER LAKE ROAD

TO BURLINGTON AND ⟨20⟩

HOST SITE

BAKER LAKE

PAY STATION

PERMIT BOUNDARY →

CAMPSITE	▲8
RESTROOM	♟♙
WATER ACCESS	🚰
PARKING	🚗
WHEELCHAIR ACCESS	♿
PICNIC AREA	⛱
GATE	⊠
BOAT RAMP	◣
TRASH	🗑
STATE RD.	⟨20⟩

Forest Service and U.S Army Corps of Engineers for restoring or preserving the rustic beauty of this modest place.

Campsites along the lake are best for privacy and proximity, but all sites are large and well spaced. The underbrush is surprisingly light, but with each site being luxuriously large, this is not a concern. Sites 5 and 6 are plum. On the loop, I would go for sites 9 or 10.

Don't confuse Panorama Point with Baker Lake Resort, a Puget Sound Energy–owned and operated facility just up the road from the Forest Service campground. In existence since the 1930s, Baker Lake Resort can be handy if you have forgotten supplies. You can buy groceries, rent a kayak, and even purchase a fishing license there.

GETTING THERE

From I-5 in Burlington, follow WA 20 east approximately 22.5 miles to Baker Lake Road (FS 11). Head north on Baker Lake Road about 18 miles and follow the signs to the campground.

SILVER FALLS CAMPGROUND

> *The Lake Chelan area, while spectacularly beautiful, is overrun with tourists; but not far away lies this uncrowded, overlooked escape.*

THIS LISTING COMES HIGHLY endorsed by a number of sources, including the manager of the state parks at Lake Chelan. That should tell you something (about Lake Chelan, at least).

In the summer, this second-deepest lake in the United States is a tourist and vacationer's mecca for just about every variety of outdoor recreation you can imagine. Campgrounds overflow week after week.

This is not to take anything away from the spectacular beauty of the area. Unfortunately, this is the wry irony of so many spots in the Northwest. Their singular and stunning scenery is what attracts people to them. Sometimes the enthusiasm gets out of hand, as with Lake Chelan, in my opinion. If you can look beyond the cluster of lakeside resorts, condominiums, and RV parks that mar the southern stretches of the shoreline, however, you will see the natural splendor of a 55-mile-long, glacier-fed lake with mountain slopes rising as high as 8,000 feet that are blanketed in aspen, cottonwood, fir, and pine.

Silver Falls Campground sits deep in the canyon-gouged Entiat River Valley in isolated splendor amid stands of cottonwood, pine, fir, and aspen. The Entiat River and Silver Creek meet at the campground, and a trail leads a half mile to the base of lovely Silver Falls. Other trailheads into the Entiat and Chelan Mountains are a short drive from the campground. At road's end (nearly 40 miles from the main highway) is another Forest Service campground and a trailhead into the wild and remote southern portions of Glacier Peak Wilderness. This is terrain for experienced backpackers only because it has steep, grueling ascents over trails of crumbling, ancient, volcanic rock. At least half a dozen peaks above Entiat Meadows are in the 7,000- to 8,000-foot range. This is the eastern edge of the Cascade Mountains, where vegetation is not as dense as on

RATINGS

Beauty: ✪ ✪ ✪ ✪ ✪
Privacy: ✪ ✪ ✪ ✪ ✪
Spaciousness: ✪ ✪ ✪ ✪
Quiet: ✪ ✪ ✪ ✪ ✪
Security: ✪ ✪ ✪ ✪
Cleanliness: ✪ ✪ ✪ ✪

the western side. Trails often traverse dry, sun-parched routes. Carry water from midsummer on, and be aware that thunderstorms can be sudden and fierce.

The landscape around Silver Falls is a contrast to that below in the town of Entiat. Fed by a glacier of the same name, Entiat River and its innumerable small tributaries are part of the water supply for a small but thriving apple industry that got its start through the perseverance of a Caribbean farmer who settled in the Entiat Valley in 1868. His first attempts to cultivate peaches and prunes failed miserably. He tried growing apples not long after, and the rest is history. The apple industry in Washington State today is one of the state's most lucrative businesses.

Continuing deeper into the valley, one finds the terraced orchards give way to the coolness of pine and cottonwood forests, with the grandeur of the rugged peaks providing a dramatic backdrop. Looking back, the rich blue-green of the Columbia, the lush assortment of fruit orchards on the benchlands, and the dry, rolling wheat fields of the eastern plateau at one glance reveal the diversity that Washington State offers travelers.

In addition to Silver Falls, Preston Falls and Entiat Falls are worthwhile side trips. Take a peek down into Box Canyon from the marked viewpoint. Mountain bikers will enjoy the network of Forest Service roads into the Entiat Valley, but be reminded that wheeled vehicles are not allowed in designated wilderness areas.

Those of you who can't resist the siren song of civilization nearby can sneak off to Lake Chelan, but don't go via FS 5900 (Shady Pass Road) even though a decent map might suggest that this is a good idea. It's longer to go back down Entiat Road, but trust the voice of experience on this one. The Shady Pass Road can hardly be considered a road—more like a very bad wagon trail. Once unknowing, I figured it for a shortcut to span the roughly 30 miles over the ridge to Lake Chelan. After traveling four-plus hours over terrifyingly rutted and rock-laden roads and through the ghoulish remains of a very devastating forest fire in the full-on heat and dust of an August day, I arrived at Chelan's shore. *Never* did two cold beers taste so good! *Never* was I so happy to still have my muffler intact.

KEY INFORMATION

ADDRESS:	Silver Falls Campground c/o Entiat Ranger District P.O. Box 476 2108 Entiat Way Entiat, WA 98822
OPERATED BY:	U.S. Forest Service, Wenatchee National Forest, Entiat Ranger District
INFORMATION:	(509) 784-1511
OPEN:	Late May or early June–October, depending on snow
SITES:	31
EACH SITE HAS:	Fire ring, picnic table, shade trees
ASSIGNMENT:	First come, first served; no reservations
REGISTRATION:	Self-registration on site
FACILITIES:	Pit toilets, centralized water pumps, disabled-access trail; 1 group site (about 30–50 people), $60 per night
PARKING:	In campground and at individual sites
FEE:	$9 per vehicle per night
ELEVATION:	2,400 feet
RESTRICTIONS:	**Pets:** On leash **Fires:** Restricted during dry seasons **Alcohol:** Permitted **Vehicles:** No ATVs in Wenatchee National Forest

MAP

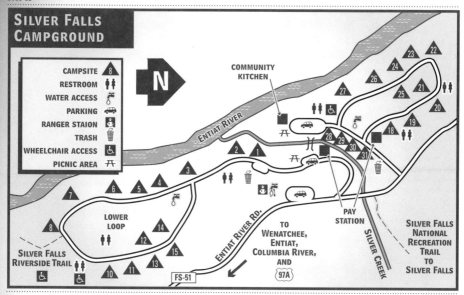

SILVER FALLS CAMPGROUND

CAMPSITE
RESTROOM
WATER ACCESS
PARKING
RANGER STAION
TRASH
WHEELCHAIR ACCESS
PICNIC AREA

N

COMMUNITY KITCHEN

ENTIAT RIVER

LOWER LOOP

SILVER FALLS RIVERSIDE TRAIL

ENTIAT RIVER RD.

TO WENATCHEE, ENTIAT, COLUMBIA RIVER, AND
97A

FS-51

PAY STATION

SILVER CREEK

SILVER FALLS NATIONAL RECREATION TRAIL TO SILVER FALLS

GETTING THERE

From Wenatchee, drive north on US Alternate 97 about 15 miles to Entiat River Road (just south of the town of Entiat). Turn left (west) onto Entiat River Road (FS 51) and drive 30 miles to the campground.

So, if you must go, leave enough time and daylight to enjoy the views on the return. Coming out of Knapp Coulee on a velvety summer evening as the setting sun casts its glow over the Columbia River in the rosy and golden hues of peach and apple country is definitely one for the picture album.

CENTRAL **CASCADES** **AND** ENVIRONS

BECKLER RIVER CAMPGROUND

YOU'VE STARTED THE DAY with a plan to leave Everett in the morning and be in Leavenworth in time for dinner by the campstove. By the time you pack the car, stop for coffee and pastries, crawl through the growing congestion of Snohomish, Monroe, Sultan, Startup, and Gold Bar (beware the speed traps in these hamlets of 25-mph zones), gawk at Mount Index, take a short leg-stretching hike to Sunset Falls, and pause to watch kayakers as they thread the boulder gardens along the Skykomish River, it's clear you won't have much daylight left to enjoy the sights, sounds, and tastes of Leavenworth. Might as well find a campground close by!

Behold Beckler River—just when you need it! This is one of the few campgrounds along US 2 between Gold Bar and Leavenworth (much of US 2 can be aggravatingly slow going because it is a winding, two-lane road where passing is suicide). Only 60 miles from Seattle, Beckler sits on the banks of the clear-running Beckler River 3 miles northeast of the historic village of Skykomish.

A heavy canopy of western Washington foliage shades the area around the campground as well as the numerous steep-sided river and creek valleys whose tributaries drain into the Beckler River. The moist climate produces tall stands of Douglas fir, western red cedar, oak, maple, and alder. At lower elevations, ferns and Oregon grape grow thick, while red and blue huckleberries can be found higher up. It's common to find skunk cabbage and trillium along the riverbeds. When I visited the campground in early fall 2003, a mushroom-hunting club was having great success quickly filling their baskets with a wide assortment of delectable fungi (and perhaps a few not-so-delectable ones as well).

The absolute best sites are along the river—4, 6, 8, and 10. The next best are 26 and 27, these being on

> *If you want a good base camp from which to daytrip into wilderness areas both north and south, enjoy hot springs and historic towns, and hike ridges and run rivers, Beckler is a great choice.*

RATINGS

Beauty: ✪ ✪ ✪ ✪ ✪
Privacy: ✪ ✪ ✪
Spaciousness: ✪ ✪ ✪
Quiet: ✪ ✪ ✪ ✪
Security: ✪ ✪ ✪ ✪ ✪
Cleanliness: ✪ ✪ ✪ ✪

ADDRESS: Beckler River Campground c/o Skykomish Ranger District Box 305 Skykomish, WA 98288

OPERATED BY: Mount Baker–Snoqualmie National Forest

INFORMATION: (360) 677-2414

OPEN: Memorial Day weekend–mid-September

SITES: 27

EACH SITE HAS: Picnic table, fire pit with grill, shade trees

ASSIGNMENT: First come, first served for 9 sites; 18 sites are reservable

REGISTRATION: Self-registration on site

FACILITIES: Vault toilets, piped water; firewood; store, ice, gas, and 3 cafés within 2 miles; public telephone

PARKING: At individual sites

FEE: $15 per night standard; $10 primitive; $5 boat moorage; $5 day-use parking (or buy an annual permit sticker)

ELEVATION: 1,000 feet

RESTRICTIONS: **Pets:** On leash
Fires: In fire pits only
Alcohol: Permitted
Vehicles: RVs and trailers up to 21 feet

the river side of the loop. After this, it's a toss-up because they are all comparable in size (huge) and privacy (respectable). If you don't have to choose 1, 2, or 3, you will not have much to complain about.

Geologically, this area has a wonderment of sharply thrusting young granite pushing up through old, decomposed and metamorphosed material. Estimates date the old rock as far back as 200 million years. A convenient place to view this clash of old and ancient is about 3 miles east of Skykomish where the Beckler Peak batholith crosses US 2. This is very close to the Straight Creek fault, which is used by geologists as the official dividing line between the eastern and western slopes of the Cascade Range.

A bit farther east is Stevens Pass, a popular ski resort in the wintertime. Once snowmelt clears the trails in summer (usually by mid-July), it is the place to catch the Pacific Crest National Scenic Trail either north or south. East to west, Stevens Pass was the route of the Great Northern Railway when it was established in the 1890s by James T. Hill. Today, the Stevens Pass Historic District preserves what is left of the track and allows visitors to explore along it. A modern railway built to parallel the old route has a significance of its own as the longest railroad tunnel (8 miles) in the Western Hemisphere.

Trips into the Beckler backcountry should be preceded by a visit to the Skykomish Ranger Station. Heavy snow often keeps trails blocked longer than one would imagine. With all the high-quality mountain terrain to traverse, it will be tempting to strike out for the nearest ridge.

The Henry M. Jackson Wilderness (named for a former Washington State senator) lies to the north. There are 49 miles of hiking trails that were once the cross-Cascade routes used by early Native Americans and later by exploration teams. Follow the Forest Service road past Garland Hot Springs to reach the trailheads.

To the south is the fabled Alpine Lakes Wilderness—roughly 300,000 acres of high-altitude meadowlands and lake basins that are the heartthrob of metropolitan Puget Sounders. In an effort to control

MAP

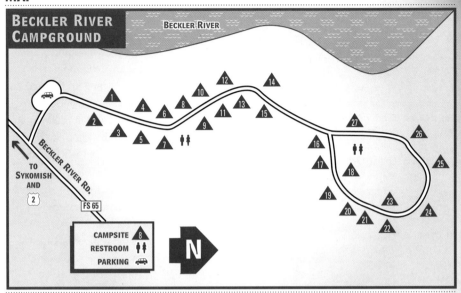

BECKLER RIVER CAMPGROUND

BECKLER RIVER

TO SYKOMISH AND

FS 65

CAMPSITE	8
RESTROOM	👫
PARKING	🚗

N

the throngs into this extremely fragile area, the Forest Service has instituted a permit system that affects even day hikers. Now you can't say you didn't know. Trailheads into the Alpine Lakes Wilderness are just west of Skykomish on Miller River Road, which becomes FS 6412.

GETTING THERE

From Skykomish, drive 1 mile east on US 2, turn left onto FS 65 (Beckler River Road) and drive 2 miles to the campground entrance on the left.

BEDAL CAMPGROUND

> *This classic riverside setting remains unspoiled despite its proximity to a popular scenic loop drive.*

YOU'VE PROBABLY DONE what I've done—driven right by Bedal on the way to loftier destinations or while out for a day cruise of the Mountain Loop Scenic Highway.

It's easy to dismiss Bedal for its proximity to this busy scenic drive that is a north–south connector within the Mount Baker–Snoqualmie National Forest. Hikers are headed east for deeper trail access points into Glacier Peak Wilderness. Mountain bikers are churning toward Monte Cristo to the south. Fishermen peel off at the White Chuck River to the north. Hedonists have heard about Kennedy Hot Springs and hope to partake of some debauchery. Families want the creature comforts of more-developed campgrounds in the Verlot stretch. RVers simply don't have enough elbow room or turning radius.

But for us tent campers, Bedal offers a classic riverside setting on the Sauk that has been unspoiled by the steady streams of passers-by. Oddly enough, Mother Nature has been the source of chaos at Bedal most recently, wreaking havoc in fall 2003 with torrential rains, slides, and high winds to the tune of $10 million damage within the Mount Baker–Snoqualmie National Forest alone. As a matter of fact, as of this writing, the Mountain Loop Highway remains closed just south of Bedal where a bridge went the way of many giant trees and tons of debris—downriver. Considering how close it is to some of the most dramatic washouts and its position along the silty banks of the Sauk River, it's astounding that Bedal survived at all.

What a shame it would have been to lose this old friend of a campground. No information I found said one way or the other, but this must have been either a Civilian Conservation Corps site or the work of miners who gave their hearts to this area more than a century ago. Reminiscent of the CCC era is a sturdy log shelter

RATINGS

Beauty: ☆ ☆ ☆ ☆ ☆
Privacy: ☆ ☆ ☆ ☆ ☆
Spaciousness: ☆ ☆ ☆ ☆ ☆
Quiet: ☆ ☆ ☆ ☆ ☆
Security: ☆ ☆ ☆
Cleanliness: ☆ ☆ ☆ ☆ ☆

that is part of campsite 18. With its moss-coated roof and old-growth timber walls, it looks like it has weathered many a rough winter and probably even more rough-and-tumble visitors. The sense of history here gave me the odd but distinct sensation that I was being watched, if that is the right word to use. I've done a lot of solo road researching in the course of updating my books, but I've never experienced quite as eerie a sense of eyes on me as I did at Bedal. I'm not sure I felt threatened—more curious and slightly fascinated. It could simply have been the presence of the many huge old firs and cedars with their shaggy limbs and lichen drapery. Perhaps it was the *shush, gurgle, slurp* of the river as it slid quietly by. Perhaps it was the lack of a breeze on a heavy late-summer day. Maybe there are just enough glimpses of soaring mountain peaks to give one a sense of being looked down on. Whatever it was, there was a certain seductive quality in the air at Bedal and that, more than anything, is why I have included it here. I hope it will be part of your experience, too.

Let me help you settle in quickly, and the choice of activity from there on out is yours—everything from the aforementioned mountain biking to just-across-the-road trekking in the Henry M. Jackson Wilderness. The campground is oval-shaped, with two sites outside the entrance and several sites flanking either side of the camp road as you enter. Unless these are your only option, head for any of the sites along the Sauk River. Following the one-way road signs, these are in order as you make your way: 16, 15, 14, 13, 12. For ultimate privacy, go for site 7 (not on the river but tucked into a thick cluster of undergrowth—maybe start your own debauchery here)! If the weather looks iffy, take site 18 and you can make money renting out the shelter for the night!

If you've come to Bedal for an extended stay, plan on at least one outing to Monte Cristo for the historical experience (check conditions here as well—floods took their toll, and rumor has it that vehicular travel is restricted). A second outing should take in some aspect of Glacier Peak Wilderness, due east as the crow flies but with trailheads possibly compromised by that nasty

KEY INFORMATION

ADDRESS:	Bedal Campground c/o Darrington Ranger District 1405 Emens Street Darrington, WA 98241
OPERATED BY:	Mount Baker–Snoqualmie National Forest
INFORMATION:	(360) 436-1155; reservations (877) 444-6777; www.reserve usa.com
OPEN:	Memorial Day weekend–Labor Day weekend
SITES:	18
EACH SITE HAS:	Picnic table, fire pit with grill, tent pad
ASSIGNMENT:	13 of 18 sites reservable; otherwise first come, first served
REGISTRATION:	Self-registration on site
FACILITIES:	Vault toilets; picnic shelter; handicap access; no drinking water
PARKING:	At individual sites
FEE:	$11
ELEVATION:	1,300 feet
RESTRICTIONS:	Pets: On leash only Fires: In fire pits only Alcohol: Permitted Vehicles: Trailers up to 21 feet long

MAP

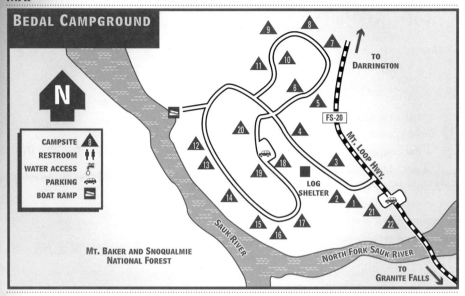

BEDAL CAMPGROUND

N

CAMPSITE	8
RESTROOM	👫
WATER ACCESS	🚰
PARKING	🚗
BOAT RAMP	

9 8
7
TO DARRINGTON

11 10
6
5
FS-20

20 4
12
18 3
13
19
LOG SHELTER
14 2 1
21
22

15 17
16

SAUK RIVER

MT. BAKER AND SNOQUALMIE NATIONAL FOREST

NORTH FORK SAUK RIVER
TO GRANITE FALLS

MT. LOOP HWY.

GETTING THERE

From Darrington, drive south on Mountain Loop Scenic Byway (FS 20) for 18 miles. The campground entrance is on the right. The roadway turns to gravel at 4 miles. As of fall 2004, the road between Bedal and Barlow Pass to the south was closed, which makes access to Bedal impossible from Granite Falls. The most up-to-date information is available on the Mount Baker–Snoqualmie National Forest Web site: **www.fs.fed. us/r6/mbs/conditions/.** This is as current as it gets.

flood business. Pugh Mountain (within view of Bedal) may be an alternative and one that will give you a very good workout as well as stunning views.

BEVERLY CAMPGROUND

Deroux C.G. - small, higher, off main rd. best in area. THfr Koppen Mt.

I T DOESN'T GET MUCH SIMPLER than Beverly. But that's okay. You won't be spending much time in the campground anyway.

As one of the more popular eastern gateways to the Alpine Lakes Wilderness, the Teanaway River valley can get a bit busy at times. Don't worry. Most of the Alpine Lakes devotees flocking en masse to its breathtaking delights have no intention of stopping at Beverly. They are beelining it to backpacking in their beloved Enchantments—in the name of preserving the environment! For this reason, the Forest Service has had to institute a permit system for all visitors to the trammeled region, and an overnight permit for six quota zones is now the practice. Imposing these restrictions brought sharp criticism initially, but it has been the only way for the Forest Service to monitor the usage of and impact on the incredibly fragile ecosystems. Had they been able to anticipate the rapid swell in the outdoor-crazed Puget Sound Basin population, I'm sure the permit system would have been introduced much sooner and saved the landscape in advance. Hindsight is bliss!

Beverly, in contrast to the beauteous heights to the west, doesn't have much to offer in the looks department, and it has even less in the way of amenities. But, to me, there is a sublime charm to places like Beverly. I like to call it the "minimalist advantage," or the "less is more" approach to car camping.

At Beverly, the immediate scenery is nothing to take your breath away. Ponderosa pine, lodgepole, larch, maybe a cottonwood or two—the usual suspects in the dry, ranchland-oriented eastern slopes of the Cascades. Campsites are spaced generously around the loop drive, which is fortunate because the sparse undergrowth doesn't afford a lot of privacy between sites otherwise. Thirteen of the sites are distinctly

> *This is the best place for a base camp into the Alpine Lakes Wilderness from an eastern approach—with crowds that pass you by.*

RATINGS

Beauty: ☆ ☆ ☆
Privacy: ☆ ☆ ☆ ☆
Spaciousness: ☆ ☆ ☆ ☆ ☆
Quiet: ☆ ☆ ☆ ☆ ☆
Security: ☆ ☆ ☆
Cleanliness: ☆ ☆ ☆ ☆ ☆

ADDRESS: Beverly Campground c/o Cle Elum Ranger District 803 West Second Street Cle Elum, WA 98922

OPERATED BY: Wenatchee National Forest

INFORMATION: (509) 852-1100

OPEN: June–mid-November, weather permitting

SITES: 16; 3 can accommodate small trailers

EACH SITE HAS: Picnic table, fire pit with grill

ASSIGNMENT: First come, first served

REGISTRATION: On site

FACILITIES: Vault toilets, no piped water

PARKING: At individual sites

FEE: $6

ELEVATION: 3,100 feet

RESTRICTIONS: Pets: On leash only
Fires: In fire pits only
Alcohol: Permitted
Vehicles: Recommended for small trailers

suited for tent campers, but three can handle RVs and trailers up to 20 feet long. There's the standard fire pit and grill with picnic table at each site. Nothing spectacular. Not at all fancy or elegant.

Okay, now stop and listen. What do you hear? Nothing, right? That's called "quiet." What do you see? Nothing, right? This is pretty much the only established campground on the Teanaway, and it's got only 16 sites. What does that tell you? It's not a place that attracts the hordes. What do you feel? Sunshine on your face? That's right—about three times as many days annually as on the west side of the mountains. How are we doing so far?

Admit it. There's a word for this experience. It's called *pleasant*. Sometimes, pleasant is good enough. We are too used to a world where superlatives have become commonplace. "Pleasant" just doesn't sound sexy. We expect the stunning, even in our campgrounds, for Pete's sake! The Alpine Lakes pictures on the Web site spoil us.

Well, I hear the fishing can be good in the Teanaway, so if that's what turns you on, go for it. For others, there are many hiking options outside the Alpine Lakes boundary that will satiate a lusty high-country appetite without forcing one to bend over backward for the permit system. If foot travel suddenly seems like more work than reward, there are outfitters who will take you into parts of the Wenatchee National Forest outback for a small fee (this assumes you are using this book to plan ahead). Mountain biking can be quite satisfying—simply cruising around the backroads that thread through the Teanaway and adjacent canyon areas. If you're feeling hedonistic, a loop drive on WA 10 between Cle Elum and Ellensburg takes in a surprisingly scenic section of the Yakima River and brings you back to the Teanaway Road by way of US 97.

The winter season up the Teanaway stays nearly as busy as summer, so you might want to put it on your list when the powdery snowfall accumulates and the sun shines even more brightly in a blindingly blue sky. An invigorating cross-country ski outing on mostly flat terrain (maybe shared with a few snowmobilers) in the cold, crisp eastern Washington air may be just the

MAP

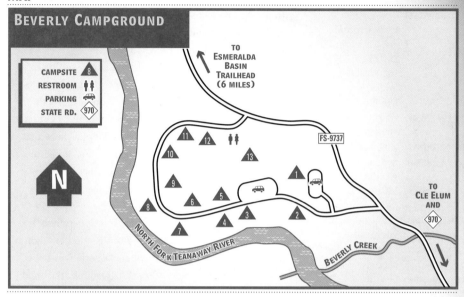

BEVERLY CAMPGROUND

CAMPSITE 8
RESTROOM
PARKING
STATE RD. 970

TO
ESMERALDA
BASIN
TRAILHEAD
(6 MILES)

FS-9737

TO
CLE ELUM
AND
970

N

11 12
10
13
9   1
8   6   5
7   4 3   2

NORTH FORK TEANAWAY RIVER

BEVERLY CREEK

occasional jolt we need to get us through that sluggish, drippy endurance test most of us call "living" between November and March.

To my mind, Beverly is the kind of campground that serves two important functions in the greater scheme of outdoor recreation: it's a reminder of the reason we go camping in the first place: simplicity, and it allows us to choose between crowded and uncrowded.

And, frankly, I think that's kind of sexy.

GETTING THERE

From Cle Elum, go 8 miles east on WA 970 to Teanaway Road. Turn left and go 13 miles to pavement's end and the beginning of FS 9737. (The road changes to North Fork Teanaway at the sharp right, swinging north into a tiny business district known as Casland before becoming FS 9737). Follow this 4 miles and the campground will be on the left.

LAKE WENATCHEE STATE PARK CAMPGROUND

> *Here's one for the entire family. It's got everything!*

ALTHOUGH IT IS QUITE LARGE, Lake Wenatchee State Park is a pretty nice spot, with spacious and secluded campsites and oodles of choices for enjoying the outdoor recreation of one of Washington State's most scenic and untainted areas.

The camp sprawls over 489 acres and is divided by the headwaters of the Wenatchee River into two camping complexes (north and south). Except for the high season (you can reserve from May through September), the sites are available on a first-come, first-served basis. I used to head straight for the north section, but as of June 2004, there are 42 new RV-oriented sites with 50-amp hookups in the north complex. To my mind, this has destroyed what used to be the underdeveloped portion of the park that was better suited to tent camping. Now I would be inclined to check out the south loop first. It's a personal choice as to which site will appeal to you, but I go for the ones that sit on the lake so that I have a view primarily of the natural *surroundings* rather than of other campers *in* the natural surroundings.

Within easy reach of Lake Wenatchee are Forest Service roads leading to two of the largest and most ruggedly beautiful designated wildernesses—Alpine Lakes Wilderness to the south across US 2 and Glacier Peak Wilderness to the northwest. There are miles of trails forming a network through both areas and into such spectacular high country that choosing a route to fit into your schedule can be a monumental task. There are any number of backpacking options that deserve at least a week.

Both wildernesses and all the area surrounding Lake Wenatchee are part of the massive Wenatchee National Forest (2.2 million acres) that stretches along the eastern crest of the Cascade Mountains from Lake Chelan south to Yakima Indian Reservation. Many thousands of years ago, the eastern edge

RATINGS

Beauty: ☆ ☆ ☆ ☆ ☆
Privacy: ☆ ☆ ☆
Spaciousness: ☆ ☆ ☆
(South campground)
Spaciousness: ☆ ☆ ☆ ☆
(North campground)
Quiet: ☆ ☆ ☆
Security: ☆ ☆ ☆ ☆
Cleanliness: ☆ ☆ ☆ ☆

of the subcontinent merged with the existing North American continent in a crush of ancient metamorphosed rock. Granite intruded at various times, and a newer cap of volcanic debris settled over the scene. The resultant topography in much of the national forest is an odd mixture of steeply upthrusting ridges with rivers falling in between, carving narrow canyons.

Lake Wenatchee itself is the source of the Wenatchee River, fed by the glaciers of Glacier Peak (the largest active collection in the continental United States). Numerous boating options are available on both Lake Wenatchee and the Wenatchee River. Canoes can be rented at the park's concession stand. Chances are you'll be sharing the waters with an assortment of other craft, ranging from fishermen in rowboats and motorized dinghies to kayaks, windsurfing boards, and maybe even a raft or two.

Past the crashing torrent of Tumwater Canyon (where you can occasionally get a glimpse of lunatic kayakers having the ride of their lives) and just east of the Bavarian-style burg of Leavenworth, the Wenatchee River becomes the most heavily rafted and kayaked stretch of water in the state. I got my whitewater-guide status on this run, like almost every other certified guide this side of Stevens Pass. It's a 21-mile potpourri of everything from lazy flat-water floats to rollicking Class IV hydraulics. Some books list a few of the rapids at Class VI! It is best—no, make that *mandatory*—to go with a commercial outfit unless you are an accomplished boater and know the river.

Other recreational opportunities span the seasons at Lake Wenatchee—the park is open year-round (with limited winter facilities). Fishing is one of the most popular summer pastimes, while autumn brings travelers into the area for the glorious display of changing colors and Leavenworth's lively Oktoberfest. In winter, snows can be heavy, and the park maintains a respectable number of trails for cross-country skiers and snowmobilers and offers the added luxury of heated restrooms and hot showers. In spring one can see the lovely apple, peach, pear, and cherry orchards

KEY INFORMATION

ADDRESS: Lake Wenatchee State Park 21588A WA 207 Leavenworth, WA 98826

OPERATED BY: Washington State Parks and Recreation Commission

INFORMATION: (509) 662-0420

OPEN: April–September; limited facilities October–March

SITES: 197; 2 primitive

EACH SITE HAS: Fire pit, grill, picnic table, trees

ASSIGNMENT: First come, first served; reservations May 15–September 15 at (888) CAMP-OUT or (888) 226-7688; $7 nonrefundable fee

REGISTRATION: Self-registration

FACILITIES: Showers, toilets, sinks; store, firewood, telephone, restaurant, playground; boat launch, boat rentals; group camp; horseback riding; nature walks; junior ranger programs; limited disabled access

PARKING: At individual sites

FEE: $12 per night ($11 September 15–May 15); $5 each additional vehicle

ELEVATION: 1,866 feet

RESTRICTIONS: **Pets:** On leash
Fires: In fire pits; restrictions based on fire hazard conditions; no gathering firewood
Alcohol: In campsites or at picnic sites
Vehicles: No RV hookups

MAP

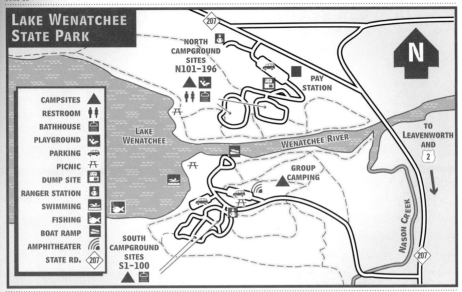

LAKE WENATCHEE STATE PARK

NORTH CAMPGROUND SITES N101-196

PAY STATION

LAKE WENATCHEE

WENATCHEE RIVER

TO LEAVENWORTH AND 2

GROUP CAMPING

NASON CREEK

SOUTH CAMPGROUND SITES S1-100

CAMPSITES	
RESTROOM	
BATHHOUSE	
PLAYGROUND	
PARKING	
PICNIC	
DUMP SITE	
RANGER STATION	
SWIMMING	
FISHING	
BOAT RAMP	
AMPHITHEATER	
STATE RD.	207

GETTING THERE

To get there from Leavenworth (23 miles west of Wenatchee), take US 2 west 16 miles to WA 207. The state park and campground are 5 miles up WA 207.

of the Wenatchee Valley in full bloom. Come back at harvest for some sampling.

Weather on this eastern slope of the Cascades is dependably hot and dry in summer and cold and dry in winter. Summer thunderstorms materialize out of nowhere, and lightning strikes can quickly ignite the forests in late summer and early fall. Be aware of the fire danger at all times, and don't discard matches or cigarette butts carelessly. Make sure they land squarely in a fire pit that's about to be doused.

Also be aware that this is bear country. Food should be stored in the car when not being consumed; a tent is not much of a deterrent to a hungry bear.

OWHI CAMPGROUND

IF THERE IS A tent camper's Shangri-la in Washington State, it would have to be Owhi.

An Indian word originally spelled Óhai and pronounced "oh high," Owhi (now pronounced ow' wee) is, as far as I know, the largest walk-in–only car-camping campground in the entire state and, without a doubt, the most idyllic. Imagine the tents as tepees and you are suddenly transported to a time that brought the tribes of the Columbia Valley to the shores of deepest-blue Cooper Lake for the abundant fishing, well-stocked berry bushes, and tranquil setting in which to commune with mountain spirits.

Looking up at Chikamin Peak and Lemah Mountain, granite fortresses guarding the magnificent Alpine Lakes Wilderness just beyond the crest of their craggy profiles, one can easily relate to Chief Owhi, a prominent Yakima tribal leader of the mid-1800s, whose passionate pursuit of the "good life" ended all too suddenly with the Treaty of 1855. Three years after agreeing to its terms but avoiding its application, Chief Owhi—who had played a relatively passive and cooperative role in the remarkably unfair exchange of land from Native American to Anglo hands—was shot to death by federal soldiers.

The passing of Chief Owhi seemed to be the straw that broke the camel's back for Washington State's Native Americans, who had aggressively opposed giving up their lands. Disillusioned and broken-spirited, they did not protest when the 1855 treaty was ratified a year after Owhi died and the peaceable easement of Native Americans from their many thousands of acres of sacred land to cramped reservations began in earnest.

Here in the serene kingdom of Chief Owhi's namesake camping grounds, your right to any of the 22 sites is denied only by your inability to get to Owhi ahead of the pack. And that can be a tough assignment.

> *Here's the ultimate tent camper's dream: a walk-in–only campground in an exquisite lakeside setting near alpine wilderness and the Pacific Crest Trail.*

RATINGS

Beauty: ✪ ✪ ✪ ✪ ✪
Privacy: ✪ ✪ ✪ ✪ ✪
Spaciousness: ✪ ✪ ✪ ✪ ✪
Quiet: ✪ ✪ ✪ ✪ ✪
Security: ✪ ✪ ✪
Cleanliness: ✪ ✪ ✪ ✪ ✪

KEY INFORMATION

ADDRESS: Owhi
c/o Cle Elum Ranger District
803 West Second Street
Cle Elum, WA 98922

OPERATED BY: Thousand Trails, under contract with Wenatchee National Forest

INFORMATION: (509) 852-1100

OPEN: Mid-June–mid-October

SITES: 22

EACH SITE HAS: Picnic table, fire pit with grill

ASSIGNMENT: First come, first served

REGISTRATION: Self-registration on site

FACILITIES: Pit toilets, boat launch, and dock; garbage dumpsters in parking lot

PARKING: In general parking areas

FEE: $8 single; $16 double; $6 for 3rd and 4th vehicle

ELEVATION: 2,800 feet

RESTRICTIONS: Pets: On leash
Fires: In fire pits only
Alcohol: Permitted
Vehicles: No trailer or pickup-camper parking

The Cle Elum River valley is less than three hours from Seattle, mostly by way of interstate, which makes it an easy mark for weekend warriors. Being at the top of the valley helps separate Owhi campers from those who are content with the more developed Wish Poosh, Red Mountain, Cle Elum River, and Salmon La Sac campgrounds that you pass on the way in.

However, there is no denying that Owhi's proximity to some of the easier eastern-access routes into the wildly popular Alpine Lakes Wilderness is its major selling point. Several trails within a mile or two of Owhi—and one that leaves right from the campground—connect to the Pacific Crest National Scenic Trail, another attraction that draws heavy crowds.

Despite all this, Owhi's primitive setup, the serenity of motorless travel on Cooper Lake, and the Panavision views right from your camp chair are incentive enough to leave the madness of the trail to the trampling throngs. If you happen to be at Owhi midweek and you're hiked out, you might feel a bit like an ostracized relative who wasn't invited to the family reunion. You could be *all alone!* In that event, pull out that novel you've been dying to delve into all summer or get out the sketchpad. There *is* life after Alpine Lakes, as it turns out.

Let's talk about the drill *before* an Alpine Lakes adventure now. A quick tour through the campground is essential on arrival at Owhi. The parking areas—split into two—are above the campsites (roughly 100 to 300 yards away). Just standing at the edge of the parking lot and trying to assess what's available will get you nowhere fast. Mainly because there's too much undergrowth between you and the campsites to see anything. Plus, while you're standing there doing your poor imitation of an Indian scout, someone else is claiming territory.

To get a feel for the variety of sites and fully appreciate how the campsites "interact," you really have to start at one end and work your way along the network of trails to the other. As you'll see, some of the sites are almost unnoticeable behind dense foliage. Others flaunt themselves. Still others are not far

MAP

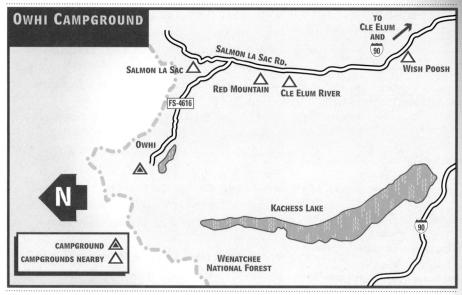

OWHI CAMPGROUND

SALMON LA SAC RD.

TO CLE ELUM AND 90

SALMON LA SAC

WISH POOSH

RED MOUNTAIN   CLE ELUM RIVER

FS-4616

OWHI

N

KACHESS LAKE

90

CAMPGROUND
CAMPGROUNDS NEARBY

WENATCHEE
NATIONAL FOREST

90

enough off the main camp thoroughfare for my taste, and then there are the double sites that have already been claimed—by the family reunions.

Still, there are plenty of sites that will please. Personally, if these are not taken, I would choose one of the sites on the southern side (18 through 22). They are at the bottom of a fairly steep drop from the parking area on a narrow, switchbacking, rooted trail (OK, even Shangri-la has its problems), and they tend to be a bit more off the beaten path.

Of course, if a lakeside site exists, do I need to tell you what to do? Try not to be too obvious about your good fortune. A simple, bloodcurdling war whoop that would make old Chief Owhi proud will do.

GETTING THERE

From Roslyn, drive 19 miles north on WA 903 (Salmon la Sac Road). Turn left onto FS 46, then go 5 miles to FS 4616 and continue for a mile to Spur Road 113. Turn left and the campground is another 300 yards. There are two parking areas; campsites are down somewhat steep trails and spread along the shore.

ROCK ISLAND CAMPGROUND

> *Grab a ticket, hop aboard, and pick your ride when you reach the end of the line at Icicle Creek.*

EVER HEARD OF THE "Rock Island Line"? Well, here's the campground personification of the railroad company that started as a one-track link and grew to control nearly all the lines in the Midwest. OK, so the comparison may be a stretch, but the name fits, and with all the spurs that lead off to interesting camping stations, it makes a good metaphor.

Actually, the campground's name comes from the very obvious landmark plunked down in the middle of the stream just above the bridge—a gigantic chunk of granite that broke off Grindstone Ridge that the creek is obliged to do-si-do around. Over eons the creek has cut quite deeply on either side of the rock, creating two narrow canyon gorges that send water shooting through in a constant, exhilarating roar. I was there in early fall of 2003 after a desperately dry summer and found that even at low water levels, there's an impressive roar. It must be a wild scene during high runoff!

There are four distinct lines that now serve the Rock Island system, but it's easy to imagine that this campground probably had modest beginnings (just like the railroad company), with three innocent sites down by the creek—sites 1, 2, and 3. Let's call this loop A (although they are not designated as such by the Forest Service). These sites sit quite exposed to the elements, mostly in full sunshine and close enough to the edge of the creek bank that taking a giant step backward could find you among the rocks below. However, loop A has the only piped water that I found, so it gets a gold star for that.

As the popularity of Icicle Canyon increased, a track pushed west, and loop B was born with six sites (4 through 9) tripling the capacity. These take full advantage of the island view and are on a knoll of pillowy, half-shaded rocks. The summer sun up Icicle Canyon can be intense, so a little shade from

RATINGS

Beauty: ✿ ✿ ✿ ✿ ✿
Privacy: ✿ ✿ ✿ ✿ ✿
Spaciousness: ✿ ✿ ✿ ✿ ✿
Quiet: ✿ ✿ ✿ ✿
Security: ✿ ✿ ✿
Cleanliness: ✿ ✿ ✿ ✿ ✿

ponderosas and firs is welcome. These are the best sites for drowning out incidental camp noise because they sit closest to the roaring surge around the "island."

Further westward expansion was inevitable, and more tracks were laid to accommodate settlement along loop C—sites 10 through 18. Timber has yet to be cleared in the hinterlands of loop C, so these sites are characterized by plenty of shade and generous undergrowth along low-bank stream frontage. I think I counted three vault toilets for nine tent sites, so the people/toilet odds are in your favor here.

A southern line came at last when funding allowed for a trestle (bridge) over the river. But the money soon ran out. Site 19 got the lion's share of space and sits in regal isolation above the creek in its own miniloop, looking down on the island across from loop B. Sites 20 through 22 would have to be considered weak attempts to continue the line (funding faltered), but they'll do if everything else is booked.

Rock Island may be at the end of the line for mechanized travel, but it is just the beginning of some glorious hiking options. This is the primary draw to Icicle Canyon (kayaking is probably the second). To the north, south, and west lies the Alpine Lakes Wilderness, acclaimed for the hundreds of places one may wander in high-country rapture even as the area desperately tries to hold up under the pressure that all its fame has put on its fragile ecosystems. Word of warning: I can't tell you not to go there (because everyone should have at least one Alpine Lakes notch on their hiking belt), but the Forest Service can! They've actually been forced to establish a lottery system for visiting certain sections of the wilderness, so read up on the restrictions before you go (**www.fs.fed.us/r6/wenatchee**). This will save major disappointment at the end of a long journey.

If you happen to get denied access, never fear. Learn more about the geology and plant life of Icicle Creek with the scenic 4.5-mile loop trail that is a gentle walk along the banks of the creek, complete with interpretive signs. The official trailhead is at Chatter Creek,

KEY INFORMATION

ADDRESS: Rock Island Campground c/o Leavenworth Ranger District 600 Sherbourne Leavenworth, WA 98826

OPERATED BY: Wenatchee National Forest

INFORMATION: (509) 548-6977

OPEN: May–October, weather permitting

SITES: 22

EACH SITE HAS: Picnic table; fire pit with grill

ASSIGNMENT: First come, first served

REGISTRATION: Self-registration on site

FACILITIES: Vault toilets; well water; garbage service

PARKING: At individual site

FEE: $10

ELEVATION: 2,900 feet

RESTRICTIONS: Pets: On leash
Fires: In fire pits only
Alcohol: Permitted
Vehicles: RVs and trailers up to 22 feet

MAP

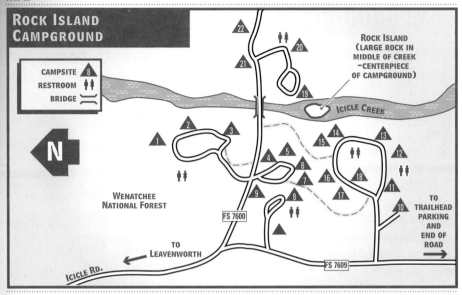

ROCK ISLAND CAMPGROUND

CAMPSITE 8
RESTROOM
BRIDGE

N

ROCK ISLAND
(LARGE ROCK IN
MIDDLE OF CREEK
—CENTERPIECE
OF CAMPGROUND)

ICICLE CREEK

WENATCHEE
NATIONAL FOREST

FS 7600

TO
LEAVENWORTH

ICICLE RD.

FS 7609

TO
TRAILHEAD
PARKING
AND
END OF
ROAD

GETTING THERE

From Leavenworth, take Icicle Creek Road south out of
town 3 miles. The road
becomes FS 7600. Drive 14
miles to the campground,
which will be on the left.
Campsites are located in
clusters on both sides of Icicle Creek and have their
own access spur roads.

but you can pick it up at Rock Island and make the full
loop from there.

Worth noting about the Icicle Creek area: forest
fires nearly made this the end of the line for good in
the past few years. You'll see evidence of the fire that
threatened Leavenworth and Cashmere on the steep
slopes above Icicle Creek. Be aware of fire-hazard levels and campfire restrictions at all times.

SODA SPRINGS CAMPGROUND

Leavenworth

FROM THE RIDICULOUS TO THE SUBLIME. This is what you'll be thinking if you choose Soda Springs Campground as an alternative to Lake Wenatchee State Park (see page 87).

While Lake Wenatchee State Park obviously has many glowing attributes and remains one of the choices in this volume, it is hardly the answer for anyone whose primary consideration in choosing a campground is seclusion. Lake Wenatchee State Park is where you go when you want a beautiful setting and are starved for companionship after a three-year stint on a deserted island.

On the other hand, Soda Springs *is* that deserted island. This is one of the tiniest, most undeveloped campgrounds you'll find in this book—and definitely within the sprawling 2.2 million acres of Wenatchee National Forest. The surprise is that only a few miles separate Soda Springs from Lake Wenatchee State Park, but the lake could easily be an ocean between the two.

Even more surprising is that Soda Springs was once sought out for the reputed healthful benefits of its waters. I haven't been able to substantiate this health claim with Forest Service personnel or history books, but a knowledgeable day-tripper insisted that this was the place. I was having a hard time visualizing this pleasant but decidedly miniscule spot handling droves of jauntily clad day-trippers in their Model Ts speeding in from Seattle to fill their water jugs. If that scene were accurate, surely some enterprising opportunist, realizing his own personal manifest destiny, would have quickly slapped a health spa on the spot and charged admission.

Today, as you enter the campground (which has a "no trailer turnaround" sign prominently placed at the entrance), a well-worn log bench is the only obvious landmark showing where the foamy upwelling (that is,

> *It's hard to imagine that this tiny, undeveloped spot was once sought out by droves of city dwellers who came to fill their jugs with its healing waters.*

RATINGS

Beauty: ☆ ☆ ☆ ☆ ☆
Privacy: ☆ ☆ ☆ ☆
Spaciousness: ☆ ☆ ☆ ☆
Quiet: ☆ ☆ ☆ ☆
Security: ☆ ☆ ☆
Cleanliness: ☆ ☆ ☆ ☆ ☆

ADDRESS: Soda Springs
Campground
c/o Lake Wenatchee
Ranger District
22976 WA 207
Leavenworth, WA
98826

OPERATED BY: Wenatchee National
Forest

INFORMATION: (509) 763-3103

OPEN: May–October,
weather permitting

SITES: 5

EACH SITE HAS: Picnic table, fire pit
with grill

ASSIGNMENT: First come, first
served

REGISTRATION: Not necessary

FACILITIES: Vault toilet; no
piped water; no
garbage service

PARKING: At individual site

FEE: No fee

ELEVATION: 2,000 feet

RESTRICTIONS: **Pets:** On leash
Fires: In fire pits
only
Alcohol: Permitted
Vehicles: No RV
turnaround (sign at
entrance)

soda) makes its appearance as Soda Creek seeps downhill to find the Little Wenatchee River. Otherwise, you'll find five very spare campsites indifferently dispersed, with one pit toilet, picnic tables, and fire rings being the only evidence that maybe someone else once washed ashore here.

Perhaps the better-kept secret of Soda Springs is found through the forest past campsite 3 on a sketchy path, over an ancient, fallen Douglas fir giant—when that tree fell, it *had* to have been heard in Los Angeles—to the rocky outcropping overlooking a dramatic sweep of the Little Wenatchee River. From here, the Little Wenatchee River plummets into Little Wenatchee Falls and flows on as the headwaters of Lake Wenatchee, which is the source of the Wenatchee River. It's hard to get away from the Wenatchee name around here.

Reflecting on the overkill of everything Wenatchee from this secret promontory, you are surrounded by the austere grandeur of true wilderness. In addition to the views below, there is a postcard scene to your left of a panorama of peaks that form the backbone of Nason Ridge. To your right is the eastern boundary of the Henry M. Jackson Wilderness as it spills over into the Wenatchee Basin. Behind you is the serpentine Wenatchee Ridge, known in literary hiking circles as Poet Ridge, which partially serves as the southeastern boundary of Glacier Peak Wilderness.

Long before these areas became protected wilderness lands, A. H. (Hal) Sylvester, the first Wenatchee National Forest superintendent, recognized that he had under his jurisdiction a whole lot of natural places that required names and he'd better come up with something a little more creative than "Wenatchee." Fully up to the task, Sylvester set about mapping the region and handing out names to reflect his classical upbringing and love of poetry. As a result, we can thank Sylvester for Minotaur Lake, Theseus Lake, and Lake Valhalla in the Henry M. Jackson Wilderness, and Poe Mountain, Irving Peak, Longfellow Mountain, Bryant Peak, and Whittier Peak in neighboring Glacier Peak Wilderness.

The Nason Ridge Roadless Area, best known for its mountain goat population and a stupendous ridgetop ramble, missed out on the poetic names with

MAP

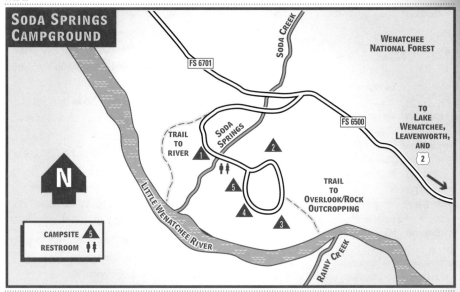

SODA SPRINGS CAMPGROUND

SODA CREEK

FS 6701

WENATCHEE
NATIONAL FOREST

TO
LAKE
WENATCHEE,
LEAVENWORTH,
AND
(2)

FS 6500

TRAIL
TO
RIVER

SODA
SPRINGS

1

2

N

5

TRAIL
TO
OVERLOOK/ROCK
OUTCROPPING

4

3

LITTLE WENATCHEE RIVER

RAINY CREEK

CAMPSITE 5
RESTROOM

more practical designations, such as Rock Mountain, Round Mountain, Mount Mastiff, Mount Howard, and Alpine Lookout. One of the few original fire lookouts in Wenatchee National Forest still in operation today, the structure hails from the Civilian Conservation Corps heyday of the 1930s.

GETTING THERE

From Leavenworth, drive west on US 2 to the Lake Wenatchee State Park turnoff (WA 207). Turn north and follow the road 12 miles, then turn west (left) onto FS 6500 and follow this 6.5 miles to the campground. Look for the "no trailer turnaround" sign at the entrance on the left. When I was there, no sign identified Soda Springs per se. A new campground has been built at Rainy Creek, but continue past this for about a mile.

SOUTHERN **CASCADES** **AND** ENVIRONS

BEACON ROCK STATE PARK CAMPGROUND

BEACON ROCK, once known as Castle Rock but renamed by Lewis and Clark in 1805, towers 848 feet above the mighty Columbia River in the Columbia River Gorge National Scenic Area and is second only to the Rock of Gibraltar in size. Several smaller but similar rock formations in this section of the gorge have prompted geologists to hypothesize that Beacon Rock may be the exposed volcanic plug of an ancient mountain, part of a range that preceded the Cascades. The monolith is estimated at 57,000 years old, actually young by geologic measure.

Apparently unimpressed by this massive adolescent of geologic time, the U.S. Army Corps of Engineers wanted to blast Beacon Rock to bits sometime around the turn of the century. Fortunately, railroad officials opposed the idea and stopped the demolition. Theirs wasn't a particularly noble reason, however. They simply didn't want rocks falling on their new tracks. Another popular idea at the time was to convert the rock into a commercial quarry.

The fate of Beacon Rock remained uncertain until 1915 when Henry Biddle bought it and proceeded to build a trail to its summit. The project cost him $15,000, a considerable sum in those days. When Biddle died, his heirs were instructed to sell Beacon Rock to the state of Washington for a mere dollar. One small restriction accompanied the low price, however. The land was to be preserved as a public park.

At first, Washington refused to honor the terms, so the Biddle family approached the State of Oregon with the same deal. An Oregon-owned park on Washington soil almost became a reality until Washington reconsidered and handed over the buck.

Today, the trail that Henry built switchbacks a dizzying 52 times to the top and crosses 22 wooden bridges. Spectacular views up and down the gorge

> *The Northwest's longest and largest river cutting a huge sea-level pass through the Cascade Mountains teams with the world's second largest monolith to produce the main attractions at Beacon Rock State Park.*

RATINGS

Beauty: ✪ ✪ ✪ ✪
Privacy: ✪ ✪ ✪ ✪
Spaciousness: ✪ ✪ ✪ ✪
Quiet: ✪ ✪ ✪ ✪ ✪
Security: ✪ ✪ ✪ ✪
Cleanliness: ✪ ✪ ✪ ✪ ✪

ADDRESS: Beacon Rock State Park
3483L WA 14
Skamania, WA 98648

OPERATED BY: Washington State Parks

INFORMATION: (509) 427-8265;
(800) 233-0321

OPEN: Park: Year-round
Main campground:
April 1–October 31;
sites near moorage
area available year-round

SITES: 29 standard; 1 primitive (walk-in)

EACH SITE HAS: Picnic table, fire grill, shade trees

ASSIGNMENT: No reservations; first come, first served

REGISTRATION: Self-registration

FACILITIES: Flush toilets, showers (for a fee); playground; dump station; boat dock, launch nearby; upper and lower shelters and kitchens; picnic and viewing area; group facilities

PARKING: At individual sites; as marked for group site; picnicking; shelter/kitchen use

FEE: $16 standard; $10 primitive; $10 minimum daily boat moorage; $5 day-use parking (except with annual permit)

ELEVATION: 700 feet

RESTRICTIONS: Pets: On leash
Fires: In fire pits only when allowed
Alcohol: Permitted
RVs and trailers: Not recommended for most sites

(including views of Oregon's Mount Hood and Washington's Mount Adams) are the reward.

Aside from Henry's mile-long piece of engineering (which is a must-see), you can follow a network of other paths throughout the park's interior to Rodney Falls and Hardy Falls. The Pacific Crest National Scenic Trail intersects the park's trail system at the northeastern corner and takes the ambitious wanderer north out of the park and into steep terrain strewn with basaltic rubble to Table Mountain (elevation 1,042 feet). If you follow the Pacific Crest Trail south, you'll come to the point where it crosses over into Oregon at a trailhead near the Bridge of the Gods (a worthwhile side trip of its own).

The hike to Hamilton Mountain is a more doable distance for most hikers. At 745 feet, it is the second-highest point in the park (Beacon Rock is first, of course). Sitting beside Hardy Falls as it tumbles down Hardy Creek, with a forested mountain at your back, birds flitting, chipmunks scurrying, and the fragrant wisps of campfire smoke wafting past combine to provide as fine a Northwest outing as anyone can hope for.

As for the camping options, the main campground is tucked against a forested hillside on the north side of WA 14. You get a taste of what lies ahead as you wind upward away from the river on the paved camp road under a thick canopy of tall trees. There are 26 sites cozily situated and generously spaced, all standard but for the first site as you enter the camp loop. This is the one primitive site, reserved for hikers and bikers. The main campground is accessible from early April to late October. Four more sites are located down by the boat launch on the Columbia and are available all year. All sites are on a first-come, first-served basis. I didn't notice any site that stood out from the others; they were equally appealing!

The good news is that the campground is primarily suited to tent campers, with narrow passage through the camp loop, a few tight turns, and limited clearance and parking discouraging the RVs. Not to mention no hookups. As a result, Beacon Rock has an air of intimate detachment. There are travelers who are passing through—just stopping long enough to restore their

MAP

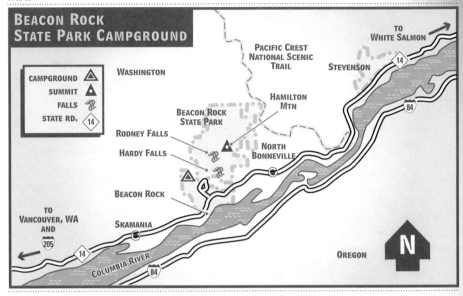

BEACON ROCK STATE PARK CAMPGROUND

CAMPGROUND △
SUMMIT ▲
FALLS 🦅
STATE RD. ⟨14⟩

WASHINGTON

PACIFIC CREST NATIONAL SCENIC TRAIL

STEVENSON

TO WHITE SALMON

⟨14⟩

⟨84⟩

HAMILTON MTN

BEACON ROCK STATE PARK

RODNEY FALLS

HARDY FALLS

NORTH BONNEVILLE

BEACON ROCK

TO VANCOUVER, WA AND
⟨205⟩

SKAMANIA

⟨14⟩

COLUMBIA RIVER

⟨84⟩

OREGON

N

---

road-weary bones by a roaring campfire. There are weekenders from Portland who have read about the glorious wildflower displays in the Hamilton Mountain meadows. There are young couples testing the camping compatibility factor in a spot not too remote. There are rock climbers who pit their skills against the face of Beacon Rock (except during the "no climb" periods when the nesting raptors are not to be disturbed).

Whatever brings you to Beacon Rock, I hope you leave with the same feeling I had—that there should be more state parks with camping areas like this one. Even the parks system recognizes its own gem—Beacon Rock State Park ranked among the "best-kept secrets" on the Washington State Parks Web site in the summer of 2004. Go soon!

GETTING THERE

From the junction with I-205 outside Vancouver, Washington, drive east on WA 14 approximately 30 miles along the Columbia River. The campground entrance will be on your left past the state park sign and park office; Beacon Rock will be on your right.

CORRAL PASS CAMPGROUND

> *Prepare for 6 miles of steep, winding dirt road. Your reward? Your own private, incredible view of Mount Rainier.*

FOR YOUR OWN PERSONAL, unsurpassed view of the north face of Mount Rainier and for a different perspective of Crystal Mountain Ski Area, take a hard left off WA 140 about 30 miles southeast of Enumclaw onto Forest Service Road 7174. This is a challenging piece of roadway that is minimally marked at the entrance.

The bumper-to-bumper traffic will go whizzing by, and you'll find yourself facing nearly 6 miles of a very steep, winding dirt route best traveled by high-clearance vehicles. No RVs to worry about here. After you've cursed me for sending you up a goat track, you'll thank me once you reach the campground.

You'll also thank me for reminding you to bring lots of water. There is none at Corral Pass. There are a few small creeks that trickle off the flanks of Mutton Mountain and Castle Mountain, but these can be unreliable in late summer or during an unusually dry season such as we've had the past few years.

Campsites are located at the end of the road that bends to the right past the intersection to the Noble Knob trailhead parking lot and through the broad, open area for horse-trailer turnarounds (not quite sure how horse trailers are able to get up there any easier than RVs, but let's not worry about it).

Continue on to the campground loop and pick from a pleasant variety of tree-shaded sites with lots of heavy vegetation between them. The camping area is small and quite undeveloped, quickly putting you in the wilderness mood. If there are "best" sites at Corral Pass, they are the ones that are set farthest from the loop road. You'll pass sites 15 through 18 on the left first, and these may well be the best choices. They sit apart from the other sites and are closer to the new vault toilet up by the main parking area. I didn't see a

RATINGS

Beauty: ✿ ✿ ✿ ✿
Privacy: ✿ ✿ ✿ ✿ ✿
Spaciousness: ✿ ✿ ✿ ✿ ✿
Quiet: ✿ ✿ ✿ ✿ ✿
Security: ✿ ✿
Cleanliness: ✿ ✿ ✿

toilet structure in the main loop, but I assume there's one to accommodate the 14 sites there.

Because of its high altitude and possible heavy snowfalls in winter, this National Forest–managed campground has a relatively short usage period—July to late September. This is also an area of unpredictable weather patterns governed by the large white snow-cone to the south (Mount Rainier, for the uninitiated). Thunderstorms can pop up in a flash as cool, moist western clouds clash with warm, uplifting breezes on the eastern slopes. Corral Pass sits nearly on the Cascade spine and gets direct hits of these conditions as they make their transitions overhead.

Hopefully, you'll enjoy less volatile weather and more than enough hiking options at Corral Pass once you've established camp. For starters, there's Norse Peak Wilderness brushing the ridgetop just east of the campground and covering more than 50,000 acres of diverse terrain dissected by 52 miles of trails. There is a surprising variety of wildlife and vegetation to enjoy as well—mountain goats, elk, and deer, to name a few. When they are in full bloom (late June to early August, depending on the elevation), the wildflowers in the meadows around Noble Knob rival those at Paradise on Mount Rainier's southern slope. Berry-picking is prime in late August and early September. Beware the competition for these from the less-than-timid bear population (sightings are becoming more frequent in the past few years, and the bears' behavior more troublesome).

A long hike that includes a bit of history and requires an overnight stay at one of several campsites along the way is the Echo Lake/Greenwater River Trail. Near the end of Greenwater is the Naches Trail, the route first used by several wagon parties in 1853. Most of the original route has long been obscured by motorbikes and jeeps that have been allowed in the area, but the still-famous "Cliff," where the pioneers lowered their wagons and horses on ropes, can be appreciated if one makes a hike down it.

Spur trails leading from Echo Lake (elevation 3,819 feet) also continue north and south to points along the Pacific Crest National Scenic Trail. From Corral Pass, a trail south stays within the Norse Peak Wilderness the

KEY INFORMATION

ADDRESS: Corral Pass Campground c/o White River Ranger District Enumclaw, WA 98022

OPERATED BY: Mount Baker–Snoqualmie National Forest

INFORMATION: (360) 825-6585

OPEN: July–late September

SITES: 26; tents only

EACH SITE HAS: Picnic table, fire grill

ASSIGNMENT: First come, first served; no reservations

REGISTRATION: Not necessary

FACILITIES: Vault toilets, firewood, horse-trailer loading ramp, hitching posts

PARKING: At individual sites

FEE: No fee

ELEVATION: 5,600 feet

RESTRICTIONS: Pets: On leash
Fires: In fire pits only
Alcohol: Permitted
Vehicles: RVs and trailers not recommended on the steep, rough road
Other: No piped water

MAP

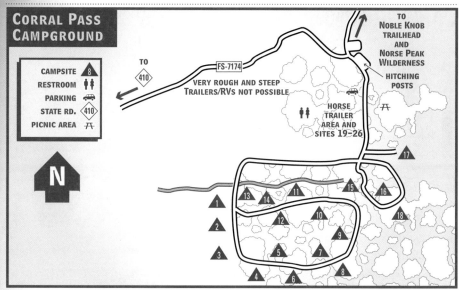

CORRAL PASS CAMPGROUND

CAMPSITE	🔺8
RESTROOM	👫
PARKING	🚐
STATE RD.	◇410
PICNIC AREA	🪧

TO ◇410

FS-7174

VERY ROUGH AND STEEP
TRAILERS/RVs NOT POSSIBLE

TO
NOBLE KNOB
TRAILHEAD
AND
NORSE PEAK
WILDERNESS

HITCHING POSTS

HORSE TRAILER AREA AND SITES 19–26

N

GETTING THERE

From Enumclaw, drive 30 miles southeast on WA 410 to FS 7174. Turn left and follow it to its end (6 miles). The highway marker for FS 7174 is on the right side of the road and is quite small. If you're at the turnoff to Crystal Mountain Ski Area or the entrance to Mount Rainier National Park, you've gone about 1 mile too far.

entire way until it hooks up with the Pacific Crest Trail at a spot known as Little Crow Basin (about 4 miles on). Several miles farther along the Pacific Crest is Big Crow Basin and views of Crystal Mountain Ski Area below. This is probably the turnaround point if you're just out for the day. Retrace your steps to Corral Pass, enjoying vistas both east and west.

GOOSE LAKE CAMPGROUND

IT WOULD BE A CRUEL HOAX to lead you into the splendid alpine world of Indian Heaven Wilderness without giving you the bad news early on.

Just when the wildflowers burst into riotous displays of color, the snow has receded from all but the uppermost hiking trails, and daytime temperatures are warming to shirtsleeve conditions, an insidious presence prevails that is the nightmare of midsummer mountain trekkers throughout much of the Northwest.

In a word, mosquitoes. You laugh. "What are a few harmless bugs?" you ask.

Well, we're not talking about the occasional little devil that wanders into your tent just as you're about to doze off and decides to make a snack of your forehead. No, we're talking about droves. Swarms. Squadrons. Plague-sized packs. There is absolutely no relief from them when they are at their worst. Even a good insect repellent is often useless.

So, armed with this knowledge, you may decide to put Goose Lake Campground on your August and September list of places to visit. Besides there being fewer mosquitoes in the higher altitudes at this time of year, there are bountiful huckleberries in late summer, and the scenery is certainly no less spectacular than in spring. Fall colors, for example, peak in late September.

Goose Lake Campground sits at almost 3,200 feet on FS 6035 about 13 miles southwest of Trout Lake. The ranger station for the Mount Adams District of Gifford Pinchot National Forest is in Trout Lake. It manages the areas around Goose Lake, including Indian Heaven Wilderness and a strange area known as Big Lava Bed. It would be a good idea to pick up road maps, trail guides, and any of the other useful information at the ranger station to get the most out of your trip. The Forest Service system of roads in these parts is a tangle of spurs off the main routes and can

> *A rustic tent-only campground that is best visited in August and September. The mosquitoes can be a nightmare earlier in the season.*

RATINGS

Beauty: ✿ ✿ ✿ ✿
Privacy: ✿ ✿ ✿ ✿
Spaciousness: ✿ ✿ ✿ ✿ ✿
Quiet: ✿ ✿ ✿ ✿ ✿
Security: ✿ ✿ ✿ ✿
Cleanliness: ✿ ✿ ✿ ✿

KEY INFORMATION

ADDRESS: Goose Lake
Campground
c/o Mount Adams
Ranger District
Trout Lake, WA
98650

OPERATED BY: Northwest Land
Management

INFORMATION: (509) 395-2501

OPEN: Mid-June–
mid-September,
depending on
weather

SITES: 18 tent sites; mostly
walk-in

EACH SITE HAS: Picnic table, fire grill

ASSIGNMENT: First come, first
served; reservations
accepted, call
ReserveUSA at (800)
280-2267

REGISTRATION: Not necessary

FACILITIES: Pit toilets, firewood,
boat ramp

PARKING: Near individual sites
and in main parking
area

FEE: $15 per site

ELEVATION: 3,143 feet

RESTRICTIONS: Pets: On leash
Fires: In fire pits
only
Alcohol: In campsite
only
Vehicles: Room for 1
trailer up to 18 feet
Other: No piped
water, no hookups

easily lead to frustration if you get adventurous off the beaten path.

The campground is a tent camper's delight, with 18 tent sites and only 1 site large enough to accommodate a small RV or trailer (up to 18 feet long). There are few trailer sites primarily because the access road is very narrow and doesn't lend itself to passage by large or wide vehicles. It's been my experience that most camp loop roads are numbered counterclockwise, but Goose Lake chooses to be different. Site 1 is to the left as you enter the compound, and site 18 comes before site 17, for some reason, as you exit the loop. All sites have views of the lake and most are walk-in as the parking area is well away from the actual campsite. Be aware that there is no piped water.

The campground attracts mainly hikers and anglers. There is a boat ramp on the lake (for nonmotorized boats only), and regular stocking with rainbow trout means good eating over the campstove. If you want to pack it in, fish, then pack it out, it's worth knowing that many of the lakes in Indian Heaven Wilderness are planted with cutthroat trout. Check with the Department of Fish & Wildlife for any current fishing restrictions.

If your interests lean toward the archaeological, Indian Heaven is a unique place for study. This high, rolling bench area between volcanoes (explosive Mount St. Helens to the northwest and Mount Adams to the northeast) once attracted Native American tribes from as far away as Umatilla and Warm Springs in Oregon. Its 175 lakes, beautiful meadows, and abundant wildlife provided Native Americans with plenty of game, fish, and berries. The Natives also indulged in one of their favorite sports in an area now called the Indian Race Track. Faint sections of the track are still evident along the southern boundary of the wilderness between Red Mountain and Berry Mountain.

Today, Indian Heaven is renowned for its huckleberry fields, and berry-picking is zealously pursued by both Natives and non-Natives. The Gifford Pinchot National Forest even maintains a "Huckleberry Hot Spots" page on their Web site. A 1932 agreement preserved a portion of the berry fields in Indian Heaven

MAP

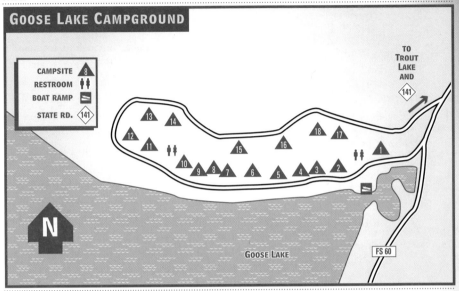

GOOSE LAKE CAMPGROUND

CAMPSITE **8**
RESTROOM
BOAT RAMP
STATE RD. **141**

TO
TROUT
LAKE
AND

141

13 14
12
11
10 9 8 7
18 17
15 16
6 5 4 3 2
1

N

GOOSE LAKE

FS 60

for Native American posterity, and there are signs indicating the reserved usage; be respectful of the tribes' berry rights.

For the geology buff, Goose Lake sits on the northern edge of the eerie Big Lava Bed. This scene resembles a moonscape. Early volcanic eruptions produced a lava flow that hardened more than 12,000 acres, leaving craters, caves, lava tubes, and other odd-shaped rock formations. The Forest Service warns that Big Lava Bed has few trails and is steep and rugged in places. If you bushwhack into the interior, keep in mind that magnetic quality of the rock surrounding you can affect the accuracy of your compass. Toward Trout Lake, Ice Caves is another unusual volcanic formation worthy of exploration.

GETTING THERE

From White Salmon on the Columbia River, drive north on WA 141 to Trout Lake (22 miles). Continue on WA 141 as it turns southwest and becomes FS 24 (Carson Guler Road) at about 5 miles. After another 2.5 miles, turn onto FS 60 and go approximately 5 miles to the campground.

LOWER FALLS RECREATION AREA CAMPGROUND

" A good site for a base camp while you explore Mount St. Helens, this area also offers major waterfall viewing and lots of other outdoor activities. "

NOT LONG AFTER the 1980 eruption of Mount St. Helens, a small plane carried its umpteenth load of international news reporters and photographers on a media junket into the area of devastation. A local reporter familiar with the Northwest terrain was among the group. As the plane flew over vast tracts of gouged landscapes and treeless mountainsides, all except the local reporter gasped and swore softly at the destruction they witnessed below them. They took copious notes and jammed camera lenses up against the plane's windows, firing off numerous rounds of film with their motor drives.

Only the local reporter sat calmly and, at one point, quietly informed his comrades that they were a long way from the Mount St. Helens zone. What they saw below, he explained, were rather typical examples of a Northwest clear-cut. They may very well have been flying up the Lewis River Valley.

I've been back up the valley several times since first writing this entry, and the old clear-cuts are starting to fill in with a soft layer of younger trees. But I still like that story and I still think the best time to head for the Lower Falls Recreation Area is about midnight on a moonless night. Now, it's not about shielding myself from the ugly clear-cutting. It's the only time I think that damn road is not full of either drivers not at all concerned about getting somewhere or drivers who are way too stressed about not getting somewhere fast enough!

Unfortunately, most of us don't want to find ourselves on a lonely stretch of backcountry roadway at midnight, so we are stuck behind each other for better or for worse. Enjoy what you can on the drive and look forward to getting to Lower Falls without undue stress. This is an area characterized by cloudy, damp weather, so if you are blessed with fewer clouds on the drive, you will see Mount St. Helens at various points

RATINGS

Beauty: ✩ ✩ ✩ ✩ ✩
Privacy: ✩ ✩ ✩ ✩
Spaciousness: ✩ ✩ ✩ ✩ ✩
Quiet: ✩ ✩ ✩ ✩ ✩
Security: ✩ ✩ ✩
Cleanliness: ✩ ✩ ✩ ✩ ✩

along the route. Some of the views are even marked. Take every opportunity you have to stop and enjoy them. Once at the falls, you'll be deep in the woods where views of mountain peaks disappear.

There in the forest the primary spectacle is a series of major waterfalls roaring off what are known geologically as "benches," wide tiers of rock formed over many thousands of years as glaciers and the Lewis River carved out the steep-sided V-shaped valley. The Forest Service has an extensive list of the waterfalls in the area, many of which are within an easy walk of Forest Service roads.

I have been to the lower of the three Lewis River Falls only at low-water times of the year—summer, to be exact. Much of the rock is exposed during low-runoff periods, but this makes for a totally different scene. The rock is worn smooth and polished, resembling a huge mass of flat-topped pillows. It is easy to imagine the thunderous splendor of these falls when water levels are high. Late spring would be the best time to see them in their glory.

Lower Falls Recreation Area has undergone some renovation recently and features twice as many campsites as before. The original 20 are still the best because they are closer to the river and have more vegetation between them, providing the ultimate in privacy. Once the new sites get some undergrowth between them, they'll be adequate. For now, let the RVs have them. Unfortunately, the trend to accommodate RVs has affected Lower Falls, and sites can now handle rigs up to 60 feet long where once they were limited to a maximum of 20 feet. Ah, the good old days.

Keep in mind that this is a campground with few amenities—only one step up from primitive. Supplies are a long way back at Cougar (and they are limited even there), so plan to go in well prepared.

Activities in the Lewis River Valley—aside from waterfall viewing—include hiking, fishing, hunting, horsepacking, canoeing, and volcano watching. There are endless trails in the neighborhood, some of which pass through the campground. The Lewis River Trail is a popular, 13.6-mile, low-elevation meander. The

KEY INFORMATION

ADDRESS:	Lower Falls Recreation Area c/o Mount St. Helens National Volcanic Monument 42218 Northeast Yale Bridge Road Amboy, WA 98601
OPERATED BY:	Mount St. Helens National Volcanic Monument
INFORMATION:	(360) 247-3900
OPEN:	Memorial Day– October
SITES:	42
EACH SITE HAS:	Fire pit, picnic table
ASSIGNMENT:	First come, first served
REGISTRATION:	Self-registration on site
FACILITIES:	Hand-pumped water, vault toilets, firewood, disabled access
PARKING:	At individual sites
FEE:	$15 per site; $5 extra vehicle
ELEVATION:	1,535 feet
RESTRICTIONS:	**Pets:** On leash **Fires:** In fire pits **Alcohol:** Permitted **Vehicles:** RVs up to 60 feet **Other:** Permits required for climbing Mount St. Helens; check Web site for latest information on volcanic activity, which may prohibit climbing, www.fs.fed.us/gpnf/mshnvm

MAP

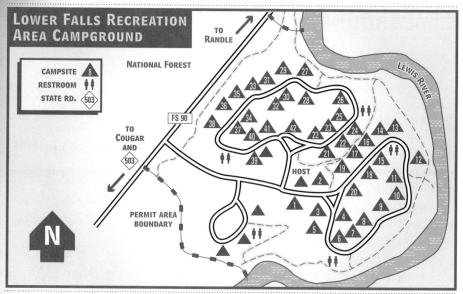

LOWER FALLS RECREATION AREA CAMPGROUND

TO RANDLE

LEWIS RIVER

NATIONAL FOREST

CAMPSITE 8
RESTROOM
STATE RD. 503

FS 90

TO COUGAR AND 503

PERMIT AREA BOUNDARY

HOST

N

GETTING THERE

Take the Woodland exit off I-5 (between Longview and Vancouver) and follow WA 503 (Lewis River Road) about 45 miles to Cougar. WA 503 beyond Cougar becomes FS 90. The campground is another 28 miles past Cougar on the Forest Service road.

river offers good trout and salmon catches at designated spots.

The Upper Lewis River canoe route can be a challenging 8 miles when heavy snowmelt turns some Class II stretches into Class IV. Check out the Mount St. Helens National Volcanic Monument Center in Swift if you are using the recreation area as a base camp to visit this modern-day geologic phenomenon. Give yourself several days just for Mount St. Helens. If you're interested in climbing the mountain, stop in at Jack's Restaurant on WA 503 west of Cougar for all the information (and permits) you'll need. At press time, Mount St. Helens is closed to climbing due to recent volcanic activity, so check the park's Web site for the latest status at **www.fs.fed.us/gpnf/mshnvm**.

MERRILL LAKE CAMPGROUND

I N MAY 1980 Mount St. Helens forever altered the landscape for miles around when it erupted in the worst natural disaster that western Washington is likely to see for a very long time. Only one other time in the recorded history of volcanic activity has a mountain exploded the way St. Helens did—more out of its side than its top. The blast (500 times greater than the force of the atomic bomb at Hiroshima) spewed billions of tons of debris northward and created a fan-shaped path of destruction that stretched over 150 square miles from northwest to northeast.

In the aftermath, St. Helens looked as if it had been savagely disemboweled with a giant scoop. Between the jagged south rim—lowered to 8,400 feet—and what was left of anything remotely mountainlike on the north rim at 6,800 feet were the remnants of the previous 9,677-foot peak. The view from the north showed a gaping amphitheater-like hollow, blackened beyond belief and measuring 1 mile wide by 2 miles long. Only seconds before, this had been a scene of tranquil, snow-capped symmetry.

Had Mount St. Helens chosen to send its pyroclastic plume in any other direction, it is highly doubtful that areas to the south (including the subject of this listing) would have been as remarkably untouched as they were. Aside from mudflows and flooding down the Kalama River, Lewis River, and Swift Creek watershed, these sections of federal- and state-managed lands sustained surprisingly little long-term damage.

In fact, campers who were enjoying the serene quiet of Merrill Lake on that fateful May morning must have been doing so with one eye nervously fixed in the direction of the mountain (which is roughly 6 air miles to the northeast). A "red zone" had recently been established for a 5-mile radius around the steaming crater, and only scientists and law enforcement officials

> *Primitive and remote, this campground south of Mount St. Helens lets you explore the area in relatively tourist-free solitude.*

RATINGS

Beauty: ✿ ✿ ✿ ✿
Privacy: ✿ ✿ ✿ ✿
Spaciousness: ✿ ✿ ✿ ✿ ✿
Quiet: ✿ ✿ ✿ ✿ ✿
Security: ✿ ✿
Cleanliness: ✿ ✿ ✿ ✿

ADDRESS: Merrill Lake
Campground
601 Bond Road
P.O. Box 280
Castle Rock, WA
98611

OPERATED BY: Washington State
Department of
Natural Resources

INFORMATION: (800) 527-3305 in
Washington; (360)
577-2025

OPEN: Memorial Day–
November 30

SITES: 8

EACH SITE HAS: Picnic table, fire
grill, tent pads

ASSIGNMENT: First come, first
served; no reserva-
tions

REGISTRATION: Not necessary

FACILITIES: Piped water, pit toilets, boat launch,
limited disabled
access

PARKING: At individual sites

FEE: No fee

ELEVATION: 1,650 feet

RESTRICTIONS: **Pets:** On leash
Fires: In fire pits
only
Alcohol: Permitted
Vehicles: RVs pro-
hibited

were allowed inside it. When the mountain blew in 1980, those lucky enough to have chosen a weekend outing on the south side probably thought that the plume of ash rising to an eventual height of 63,000 feet was the extent of the show. It wasn't until they returned home later that evening that television news reports would show them the full extent of the horror.

Today, more than two decades later, Merrill Lake Campground remains in wooded isolation just outside the boundaries of Gifford Pinchot National Forest and Mount St. Helens National Volcanic Monument. Recreational options around Merrill Lake include hiking on high- and lowland trails, boating, fishing, mountain biking, cross-country skiing, and caving.

The campground underwent a substantial facelift after the flood of 1996, which gave the DNR justification for addressing such needs as ADA compliance, adding new tent sites, upgrading existing sites, improving road conditions and the boat launch area, and making general cosmetic enhancements. Those who had had a love affair with Merrill Lake before will still be enamored of it. The same familiar rusticity, but better.

Just for the record, Merrill Lake is a favorite among DNR staff. That counts for a lot in my book!

In summer, most of the tourist throngs inundate Mount St. Helens from the north, leaving you to explore lands around the geologic wonder in relative solitude. Short drives up Forest Service roads lead to such interesting natural features as Ape Cave, a 2-mile lava tube that is representative of past volcanic activity. On the road to Ape Cave is the Trail of Two Forests, a self-interpretive walk over a 2,000-year-old lava bed. A short way up FS 24, which heads north from Lewis River Road at the east end of Swift Creek Reservoir, is the trailhead to Cedar Flats. This is a looped stroll through old-growth Douglas fir in Cedar Flats Northern Research Natural Area. These are wintering grounds for Roosevelt elk.

If you're into some serious driving and want the best views of the Mount St. Helens devastation, take FS 25 north to its intersection with FS 99. This route takes you deep into the area of destruction to a viewpoint at Windy Ridge. These Forest Service roads are

MAP

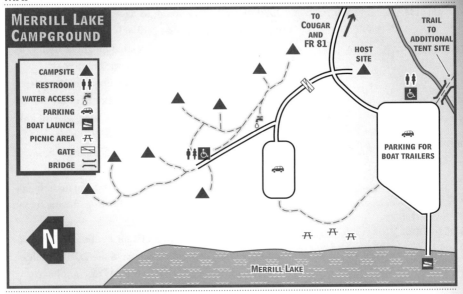

MERRILL LAKE CAMPGROUND

TO COUGAR AND FR 81

TRAIL TO ADDITIONAL TENT SITE

HOST SITE

CAMPSITE
RESTROOM
WATER ACCESS
PARKING
BOAT LAUNCH
PICNIC AREA
GATE
BRIDGE

PARKING FOR BOAT TRAILERS

N

MERRILL LAKE

gravel, and sections are closed in winter. For full information on traveling either by foot or car in Mount St. Helens National Volcanic Monument, it is best to contact the park directly for current conditions. There is a park visitor center in Swift.

GETTING THERE

Take Lewis River Road east from Woodland off I-5 to the small settlement of Cougar. Turn north, away from Yale Lake, onto FS 81, and travel 4.5 miles to the access road that leads to the campground.

MORRISON CREEK CAMPGROUND

The south face of "The Forgotten Mountain" hovers invitingly within arm's reach of this unforgettable camp in the Gifford Pinchot National Forest.

WHOEVER FIRST misrepresented Mount Adams as the "The Forgotten Mountain" must have been working for Mount Rainier National Park and never camped at Morrison Creek. Once you've been here, you're more likely to go away thinking "unforgettable" is the better description.

This is one of those rare spots that offers you a vantage point to Washington's second-highest volcano (Mount Rainier is highest at 14,410), unequaled anywhere within car-camping range (except perhaps at Cold Springs just up the road, but that's overrun with the South Climb crowd and no place for a quiet break).

When I visited in midsummer 2004, Morrison Creek was undergoing a facelift, with new fire grills, a new vault toilet, downed timber being cut up and carted away, and a few new picnic tables. Obviously, this leads me to believe that maybe Morrison Creek is being spiffed up to handle the overflow from Cold Springs. At the moment, there is no fee, but I won't be surprised to see a pay station the next time I go.

Fee or no fee, in a hot, dry stretch of prime tent-camping weather, there were only 2 of a total 12 sites taken (none of which are suitable for RVs or trailers). The feeling was distinctly one of blissful isolation. All but two of the sites (no site numbers at rustic Morrison Creek) are outside the loop drive and spaced well enough apart to ensure privacy campside. The vegetation is mainly an assortment of lofty conifers, the occasional hardwood, and shrubby huckleberry, with low-profile grasses and horsetail along the creek bed. A special feature of the natural landscaping is the elegant beargrass that grows throughout. Get a permit from the ranger station; only about 3,000 folks get in—they made this the third-highest "special forest products" revenue producer in 2003 for the Gifford Pinchot National Forest. Talk about unforgettable!

RATINGS

Beauty: ✿ ✿ ✿
Privacy: ✿ ✿ ✿ ✿
Spaciousness: ✿ ✿ ✿ ✿ ✿
Quiet: ✿ ✿ ✿ ✿ ✿
Security: ✿ ✿ ✿
Cleanliness: ✿ ✿ ✿ ✿ ✿

A live memento in the backyard is the best tribute possible.

You get more than just a hint of all that awaits you at Morrison Creek as you drive up from tiny Trout Lake (the closest depot for supplies, by the way, and home to the ranger station). The full glory of the Mount Adams landscape—a layered cornucopia of textures, colors, and altitudes—literally fills the windshield and makes the task of keeping eyes on the road a tough one. It appears that you are on a collision course with the massive glacier-clad snowcone, and it's only when you begin a noticeable altitude gain and enter the subalpine zone that views disappear just as noticeably. Don't worry. There's more where that came from farther along!

Mount Adams has been a berry-picking destination for Native Americans for roughly 9,000 years. Klickitat legend paints a colorful story of Pah-to (as Mount Adams was known to them) as a high-maintenance wife of the Sun who had a hard time staying out of trouble. Her spunky survival tactics won her more admiration than disgrace, apparently. Today, Mount Adams is considered sacred ground by local tribes who reside within its shadow on the Yakama Indian Reservation (the largest of Washington's reservations but still miniscule compared to the lands the tribes once roamed freely).

The suppression of Natives quickly led to settlement in Klickitat and White Salmon country. The open range of the Columbia Gorge highlands suggested to early settlers that cattle herding would be a profitable pursuit. But severe winters took their toll on the defenseless herds, which led to an epiphany that maybe sheep ranching was the ticket. By the turn of the century, the lower slopes of Mount Adams (including the area around Morrison Creek) saw thousands of the woolly lawnmowers munching contentedly. Sheep ranching was common in the area until the 1970s when it started to be slowly replaced by various forms of farming. Wheat took hold farther east, but the road between Trout Lake and the town of White Salmon on the Columbia is a mix of the apple, pear, and peach orchards that, with a burgeoning interest in vineyards, form the cornerstone of today's local economy.

KEY INFORMATION

ADDRESS:	Morrison Creek Campground c/o Mount Adams Ranger District 2455 WA 141 Trout Lake, WA 98650
OPERATED BY:	Gifford Pinchot National Forest
INFORMATION:	(509) 395-3400
OPEN:	July–October, weather permitting
SITES:	12
EACH SITE HAS:	Picnic table, fire ring with grill
ASSIGNMENT:	First come, first served
REGISTRATION:	Not necessary
FACILITIES:	Vault toilets, no piped water
PARKING:	At individual site
FEE:	No fee
ELEVATION:	4,665 feet
RESTRICTIONS:	**Pets:** On leash **Fires:** In fire rings only **Alcohol:** Permitted **Vehicles:** RVs and trailers not recommended

MAP

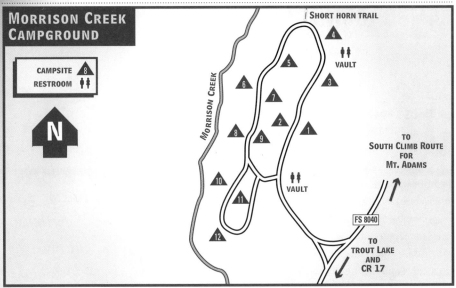

MORRISON CREEK CAMPGROUND

CAMPSITE **8**
RESTROOM **♦♦**

N

MORRISON CREEK

SHORT HORN TRAIL

4
5
VAULT **♦♦**
6
3
7
2
8
1
9

TO
SOUTH CLIMB ROUTE
FOR
MT. ADAMS

10
VAULT **♦♦**
11

FS 8040

12

TO
TROUT LAKE
AND
CR 17

GETTING THERE

From Trout Lake, drive north on CR 17 (Mount Adams Recreation Area Road) for 2 miles. Stay to the left (north), picking up FS 80 for 3.5 miles. Continue another 6 miles north on FS 8040 to the campground on the left.

Recreationally, the region is silly with opportunity, and the list is as endless as the variety is extensive— mountain biking, lava-bed exploring, berrypicking (check out the Forest Service's Web page on this), fishing, photography, scenic driving, wildflower identification, and wildlife viewing, and skiing (in winter), to name a few. Of course, with two of only three wild and scenic rivers in Washington State flanking Mount Adams through high meadows, grassy ranchlands, and basalt-walled canyons, boaters have found the ultimate challenge in both the White Salmon and the Klickitat.

Last, it almost goes without saying that hiking and mountain climbing are king in the Mount Adams Wilderness. Take the less-traveled Short Horn route right from Morrison Creek and you'll be headed for high-country adventures that can be described only as, well . . . unforgettable.

TAKHLAKH LAKE CAMPGROUND

JUST IMAGINE: you're sitting in your campsite at Takhlakh Lake gazing out at a picture-perfect view of Mount Adams. It seems near enough that you could reach out with a paintbrush to add a little more white here, a little more blue there. A living canvas right at your fingertips.

If you've forgotten your paint set, however, make sure you capture at least a scene or two on film. This is one of those spots that simply begs to be documented. On a calm and clear early morning, there can be two views of the mountain—the real-life one and the one that is a mirror reflection in the lake. Definitely worth a frame or two.

There is no easy way to get to Takhlakh, which is part of its appeal and what makes it worthy of inclusion in this book. The confusing network of Forest Service roads can be downright irritating, too, if you don't have a good map of the area. I was beginning to feel like a rat in a maze after a while. It's a good idea to stop at the ranger station either in Randle to the north (the preferred route) or Trout Lake to the south. Pick up maps, trail information, and backcountry permits.

Don't expect views of Mount Adams along the way to guide you. Except for a few stellar vistas across open farmlands as you head north from Trout Lake, say good-bye to the views until you are lakeside. These are the heavy alpine and subalpine timberlands of Gifford Pinchot National Forest. You don't want to spoil the surprise that awaits you at the lake, anyway. Besides, you'll be too busy making sure you're still on the right road (FS 23) as it wends its way through dense stands of trees, deceptively gaining altitude before reaching Takhlakh Lake at 4,400 feet.

Most of the 54 tent sites offer superb views of the lake and the mountain through stands of Douglas fir, Engelmann spruce, pine, and subalpine fir. The main

> *There are many camping options in this lake-studded sector of Mount Adams's northwestern flank, but none are quite so breathtaking as this when the mountain is in view. It's hard to get to but worth it.*

RATINGS

Beauty: ✿ ✿ ✿ ✿ ✿
Privacy: ✿ ✿
Spaciousness: ✿ ✿ ✿
Quiet: ✿ ✿ ✿ ✿ ✿
Security: ✿ ✿ ✿ ✿
Cleanliness: ✿ ✿ ✿ ✿

camping area is to the right as you drive in off the spur road from FS 23. These sites will be taken up quickly by the RVs and trailers, but if you can find a spot lakeside and far enough off the loop, go for it. The camp host's post is prominently situated in the first site as you drive in, so if you have any questions, stop right there and ask.

An attractive new feature is the walk-in tenting section to the left as you come in off the spur road. There seemed to be more cars than there were campers, but it may be that the parking area is a bit small for the number of sites there—ten in all, numbered 45 through 54. They are fairly close together—I find this is a common practice with most tent-only areas. Do car campers seem more inclined to experience a certain camaraderie in close quarters, or is it just a matter of available real estate? I wonder . . .

If you've come in search of lazy fishing opportunities, Takhlakh is a treat. Only nonmotorized boats are allowed on the glassy waters. With an Ansel Adams–like scene at your back, cast your line and wait for the trout lurking in the frigid glacial depths to find you.

For those with more ambitious recreational intentions, Mount Adams Wilderness is only minutes away. Trails lead ever higher as views of Washington's second-highest volcano get better and better with every step. Wildflowers carpet the higher meadows with bursts of color throughout late spring and early summer. Birds are plentiful and diverse. Wildlife runs the gamut of deer, marmots, squirrels, chipmunks, bobcats, elk, and moose.

A section of the Pacific Crest National Scenic Trail passes Mount Adams on the western edge of the wilderness and is accessible from trailheads near Takhlakh. Climbers also use these routes to reach Mount Adams's summit. It is possible to use Takhlakh as a base camp for extended forays around Mount Adams on what is known as the Highline Trail. This is a rigorous navigation of 90 percent of the mountain. The last 10 percent would challenge even a mountain goat. Check with a ranger before tackling this.

While the spring and summer flower displays on Mount Adams can be inspiring, their loveliness is often

MAP

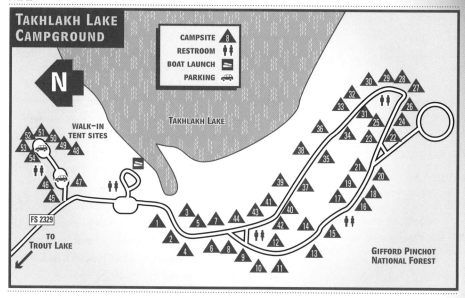

TAKHLAKH LAKE CAMPGROUND

CAMPSITE 8
RESTROOM
BOAT LAUNCH
PARKING

N

WALK-IN TENT SITES

TAKHLAKH LAKE

FS 2329

TO TROUT LAKE

GIFFORD PINCHOT NATIONAL FOREST

offset by unwelcome visitors: mosquitoes. Although they vary from year to year, late summer and early fall are predictably the best times to avoid the pesky varmints altogether. I recommend the window between late August and early October for avoiding the crossfire (literally) of hunting season that follows soon after. Autumn colors make glorious photo opportunities in October, whereas huckleberry season usually peaks by late August.

GETTING THERE

Take CR 3 off WA 12 at Randle. Go south 2 miles to FS 23. After 29 miles, turn north onto FS 2329. The campground is a little over a mile in.

To get there from Trout Lake, take FS 80 north to its intersection with FS 23. The campground is nearly the same distance as from Randle, but the road twists and turns and has vaguely marked intersections. The turnoff onto FS 2329 will be to the right coming from Trout Lake.

NORTH CENTRAL
WASHINGTON

COLD SPRINGS
CAMPGROUND

IT TOOK ME MORE THAN a year and a flurry of rescheduling over the course of many weeks late in the summer and early fall of 2004 to get here, but I finally made it to Cold Springs Campground.

Well worth the effort—but that should tell you something about your own plans to seek out this retreat high above the Sinlahekin Valley with its own viewing platform and fresh, piped spring water.

This is not a place you will ever find by accident—unless you happen to be an out-of-luck miner hanging around the Loomis Post Office waiting for the Pony Express to arrive with the latest batch of letters from back East!

Mining was what initially brought white settlers into the Sinlahekin Valley; homesteading soon followed and that was the beginning of all the trouble. Okanogan Natives had been farming and hunting undisturbed on their ancestral lands for hundreds of years. Once the word got out in the mid-1880s that there might be riches in the hills and along the river bottoms, prospectors arrived and began staking arbitrary claims, much to the dismay of the Natives. A sort of land tug-of-war began that ultimately favored the whites, and the Natives were forced to accept miniscule plots of land to stay or be relocated to the Colville Reservation across the Okanogan River. In their minds, it was a no-win situation. They were right.

The only poetic justice for the Okanogan Natives may be that very few fortunes were made in this region through mining. Eventually, interests turned to the agricultural benefits of a land that is blessed with near-perfect combinations of climate, soil, and geography for growing fruit, particularly apples. By the late 1800s, the Okanogan Valley was being recognized as one of the primary apple-growing regions in the world, and the towns along its banks thrived, whereas Loomis

> *Cold Springs is high above the Sinlahekin Valley, with its own viewing platform and fresh, flowing spring water just a few miles from the Canadian border.*

RATINGS

Beauty: ✩ ✩ ✩
Privacy: ✩ ✩ ✩ ✩
Spaciousness: ✩ ✩ ✩ ✩ ✩
Quiet: ✩ ✩ ✩ ✩ ✩
Security: ✩ ✩ ✩
Cleanliness: ✩ ✩ ✩ ✩ ✩

ADDRESS: Cold Springs
Campground
c/o Northeast
Region Office
P.O. Box 190
225 South Silke
Road
Colville, WA 99114

OPERATED BY: Washington State
Department of
Natural Resources

INFORMATION: (509) 684-7474

OPEN: All year, weather
permitting

SITES: 5 tent sites

EACH SITE HAS: Picnic table, fire pit
with grill

ASSIGNMENT: First come, first
served

REGISTRATION: Not necessary

FACILITIES: Vault toilets; piped
spring water; picnic
area; picnic viewing
platform; no
garbage service

PARKING: At individual site

FEE: No fee

ELEVATION: 6,200 feet

RESTRICTIONS: Pets: On leash
Fires: In fire pits
only
Alcohol: Permitted
Vehicles: Trailers not
recommended on
access road
Other: Pack out
trash

took a back seat—and stayed there. Today, Loomis is a quiet, unassuming gateway to the recreation areas of the Sinlahekin and Similkameen Rivers, with very little physical evidence of its boom years.

As for Cold Springs Campground, there is no overwhelming draw that puts this place on the map—and believe me, very few maps identify it—other than that it is very high and very remote. It's a backdoor view into the endless terrain of the Pasayten Wilderness to the west, a soulful reflection northward to Snowshoe Mountain, and a sidelong gaze east to Chopaka Mountain. Perhaps the best part of the trip to Cold Springs is on the descent (make that plummet) when the entire panoply of Okanogan geologic time is laid out before you in IMAX theater scale.

Unlikely as it will seem once you make your way to Cold Springs, the Department of Natural Resources has gone out of its way to maintain this lofty perch within the Loomis State Forest on one level and not on another. You will climb steadily from the Toats Junction for nearly 2,000 feet in just more than 5 miles, passing through larch and ponderosa pine forests. You'll come to the official campground on the left at about the 4.5-mile mark. You can either park here and stroll the rest of the way on foot or continue the tour by car for another half mile to the picnic area. Here, the DNR has laid a wide, smooth, curving, and accessible trail up to a concrete-slab platform with one lone picnic table—great for viewing the sunset. Someone at the DNR has a soft spot for romantic settings.

In contrast to this surprising display of agency fastidiousness, it's clear that the emphasis is on picnicking and smooching rather than camping. A number of abandoned sites dot the landscape up around the viewing area, and one undesignated site just off the parking area appears to get used once in a while. Except perhaps in a howling wind, this spot would do quite nicely, situated as it is near the view.

Down below, there are three sites that are really just part of one large cleared lot, but they have three equidistantly spaced fire rings and parking spurs on three sides. The "spring" of Cold Springs is across from site 3, and although it would probably be safe to

MAP

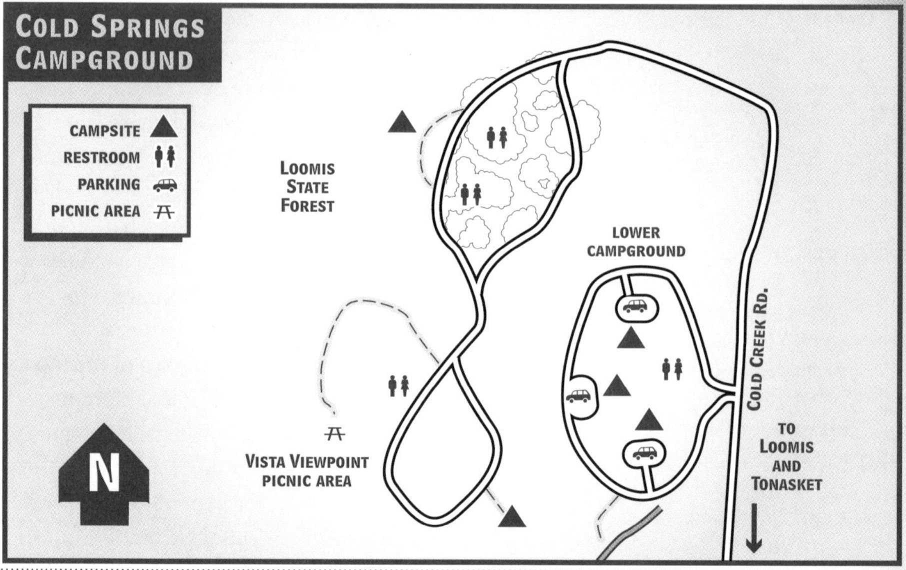

COLD SPRINGS CAMPGROUND
CAMPSITE
RESTROOM
PARKING
PICNIC AREA
LOOMIS STATE FOREST
LOWER CAMPGROUND
COLD CREEK RD.
TO LOOMIS AND TONASKET
VISTA VIEWPOINT PICNIC AREA
N

drink straight from the pipe, the DNR calls it "non-potable" water, so I guess we'd better trust them.

The main activity at Cold Springs is on the ridges and slopes within view of the "lover's loft"—hiking, in other words. There are some dandy loop trips and vista scrambles in this mostly roadless area, and any number of extended trips can start from Cold Springs if the Pasayten Wilderness is your destination. Be aware that one chunk of the State Forest is off-limits as a designated natural preserve.

To get there, make sure you have the DNR map of Loomis State Forest with you. This is the only map I've found that has Cold Springs marked on it.

GETTING THERE

From the Loomis Post Office (northwest of Tonasket), take the Loomis–Oroville Road north 2 miles to Toats Coulee Road (AKA the Chopaka Lake Road). Turn left and continue 5.5 miles to Toats Junction and the intersection of OMT 1000 and OMT 2000. Take OMT 1000 another 2.1 steep miles, then turn right on Cold Creek Road and go 0.4 miles. Keep right for 1.8 miles, then stay left and continue another 2.3 miles to the campground. The picnic area and viewpoint are a half mile up.

COTTONWOOD/ SALMON MEADOWS CAMPGROUNDS

> *Take your pick between an intimate streamside setting or lovely, large walk-in sites with freestanding river-rock fireplaces.*

TRAIPSED AROUND the Okanogan Valley and heights for several days before I got a look at Cottonwood and Salmon Meadows. Cottonwood in particular had been recommended to me by the staff at the Tonasket Ranger Station, but I was having trouble getting over there as I kept running into dead ends elsewhere that were costing me valuable time. I was a doubting Thomas about both Cottonwood and Salmon Meadows simply because I assumed that anything this close to Conconully State Park (a nice place to visit, but I wouldn't want to camp there) would be nothing but the overflow of the overflow, the worst of the worst. Disgruntled campers grousing about not having a hot shower or a place to get a pizza. I had already been horribly disillusioned by Tiffany Spring, which I had built up in my mind as a magical high-altitude kingdom and which turned out to be just a dull collection of dusty sites at a bend in the road. I tried to find Crawfish Lake the back way and wasted an entire half-day *not* getting there. I learned that Summit Lake would not be a wise choice. I wasn't in the mood for any more "thumbs down" revelations.

Well, in the words of someone who is often mistakenly identified as a relative of mine (Gomer Pyle), "Surpriiise! Surpriiise! Surpriiise!"

Cottonwood and Salmon Meadows, in their own ways distinct and about as opposite as any two campgrounds can be, proved to be gems in the rough and secured their inclusion in this book just in the nick of time. It helped that I came upon them well into the fall, which is something to keep in mind if you plan to join the fray in high season.

You may find that, of the two, Cottonwood has proportionately more room available than Salmon Meadows. With only four sites at Cottonwood, I can understand that you would look askance at me, but

RATINGS

Beauty: ✿ ✿ ✿ ✿
Privacy: ✿ ✿ ✿ ✿ ✿
Spaciousness: ✿ ✿ ✿ ✿ ✿
Quiet: ✿ ✿ ✿ ✿ ✿
Security: ✿ ✿ ✿
Cleanliness: ✿ ✿ ✿ ✿ ✿

you only have to drive down into the campground once and you'll know what I mean. It's a short, steep drop off FS 38—not at all forgiving of RVs and truck/trailer combinations that have too much length and not enough give. And once they're down there, they have nowhere to go. Each of the four sites sits quite privately from the other in a strip along the North Fork Salmon Creek on land that has been used economically and not been designed for hulking RVs. Oriole and Kerr, farther up the road, answer this need quite nicely.

Cottonwood is also the first campground up the Salmon Creek Road. While other campers are hurrying to bury themselves as deeply as possible into the Okanogan mountain experience, your choosing Cottonwood relieves you of the burden of waiting until it's too late to find a campground before nightfall. Cottonwood is often viewed as not being far enough away from the "city lights" of Conconully to earn respect as a true camping experience but, hey, when the lights go out at Cottonwood, it's just as dark as the "official" wilderness many miles away.

Salmon Meadows, in the higher reaches of North Fork Salmon Creek, could reasonably be described as a "camping village." True to its name, it occupies what I would actually call a "wooded meadow" (if that makes sense) at the confluence of two Salmon Creek tributaries, Meadow and Mutton Creeks. Here, the land flattens to a broad plain at 4,500 feet before sharply rising within several quick miles to heights above 8,000 feet at Tiffany Mountain (seen as you are crossing the meadow on FS 38 toward the campground entrance).

Upon entering Salmon Meadows, the lane passes a small shelter and pay station before rising abruptly to level out just as you get the first glimpse of the village—an impressive octagonal log shelter with a river-rock chimney and fireplace. City hall! Continuing on the camp road, sites 1, 2, and 3 are placed on the cul-de-sac, but they are not too close to one another. Life in the suburbs. It's not until you get around the far end of the loop and have started back toward the entrance that

KEY INFORMATION

ADDRESS: Cottonwood/Salmon Meadows c/o Tonasket Ranger District 1 West Winesap Tonasket, WA 98855

OPERATED BY: Okanogan National Forest

INFORMATION: (509) 486-2186

OPEN: Late May–October (weather permitting)

SITES: 4 at Cottonwood; 9 at Salmon Meadows

EACH SITE HAS: Picnic table, fire pit with grill

ASSIGNMENT: First come, first served

REGISTRATION: On site

FACILITIES: Vault toilets; artesian and hand-pumped water; garbage service at Conconully

PARKING: At individual site

FEE: $5 both campgrounds

ELEVATION: Cottonwood: 2,700 feet; Salmon Meadows: 4,500 feet

RESTRICTIONS: Pets: On leash Fires: In fire pits only Alcohol: Permitted Vehicles: Trailers and RVs not recommended at Cottonwood; up to 24 feet at Salmon Meadows Other: No RV hookups at Salmon Meadows

MAP

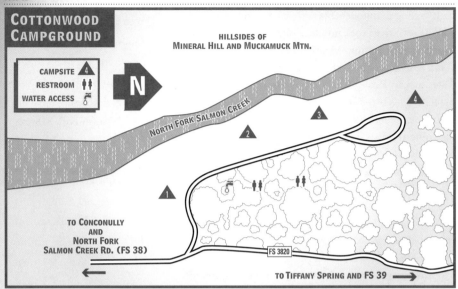

COTTONWOOD CAMPGROUND

HILLSIDES OF
MINERAL HILL AND MUCKAMUCK MTN.

CAMPSITE
RESTROOM
WATER ACCESS

N

NORTH FORK SALMON CREEK

4
3
2
1

TO CONCONULLY
AND
NORTH FORK
SALMON CREEK RD. (FS 38)

FS 3820

TO TIFFANY SPRING AND FS 39

MAP

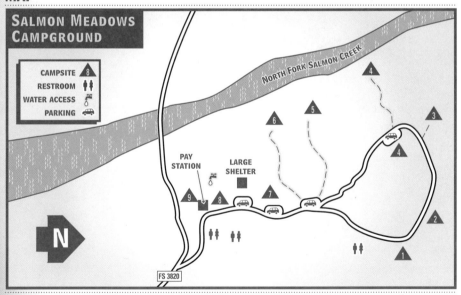

SALMON MEADOWS
CAMPGROUND

CAMPSITE
RESTROOM
WATER ACCESS
PARKING

NORTH FORK SALMON CREEK

4
6
5
3
4

PAY
STATION

LARGE
SHELTER

9
8
7
4
2
1

N

FS 3820

the most desirable side of Salmon Meadows reveals itself. Sitting in untouchable walk-in splendor—each with its own river-rock fireplace—are sites 4, 5, and 6. The Estates of Salmon Meadows. Back by city hall, sites 7 and 8 anchor either side and guard the hand-pumped water supply. Public Works Department. Police Department. Site 9 sits outside the main camping area, alone and unprotected where FS 3820 turns sharply toward the western ridges. Low-income housing?

This area of the Okanogan Highlands is rich with every recreational opportunity imaginable. Hiking ridgetops. Mountain biking on designated trails. Fishing in exquisite alpine lakes. Horsepacking into the heart of the wilderness. Gamebird hunting on wildlife refuges. Tracing local history. Analyzing geologic events. The list is truly endless.

Cottonwood and Salmon Meadows campgrounds are good places to begin the adventure.

GETTING THERE

From Omak, take the Conconully Road northwest out of town for 17.5 miles to the tiny resort village of Conconully. Continue north on FS 38 (North Fork Salmon Creek Road) for barely 2 miles to Cottonwood. To reach Salmon Meadows, continue another 6 miles past Cottonwood. You'll pass two other campgrounds, Oriole and Kerr, along the way. FS 38 becomes FS 3820 past Cottonwood.

CRAWFISH LAKE CAMPGROUND

This is a pretty spot that is shared by campers, private landowners, and the Colville Indian Nation—and it's free!

HERE'S ONE THAT HAS all the makings for being a fairly busy campground in the summer months, so you may want to put it on your agenda for when those still-warm days and crisp nights of autumn are upon us. Chances are good that you'll have the place to yourself.

Crawfish Lake is an odd mixed-use spot mainly because it has several different groups vying for its attention. On the northeastern shore are the campers enjoying their Forest Service campground with 19 very large and handsome tent sites, all of which have views of the lake, with about half the sites on its shoreline. The camp road enters the compound from the north side, allowing only sites 1, 2, and 3 to be placed around the loop at that end. The rest of the sites are staggered on either side of the camp road where it parallels the waterline and circles around a respectful distance from the reservation's boundary, giving sites 13 and 14 their fair share of space. A stand of ponderosas and larch serve as the natural buffer between federal and tribal lands, much more tasteful than an intrusive "no trespassing" sign might be. The conifers don't grow particularly thick here, but they balance the grassiness of the campsites. The general feel is one of openness and breeziness as the sun reflects brilliantly off the blue, blue water, sending a rich radiant glow in all directions.

On the far northwestern shore are the permanent homes and recreational cabins of private property owners, with manicured lawns down to the water's edge and personal boat docks. I'm sure they find the off-season the most enjoyable, too. Best not to get too curious over there.

Halfway along the lake, the property line changes to Indian ownership because Crawfish Lake has the unique honor of being split in two by the northern

RATINGS

Beauty: ✪ ✪ ✪ ✪ ✪
Privacy: ✪ ✪ ✪ ✪
Spaciousness: ✪ ✪ ✪ ✪ ✪
Quiet: ✪ ✪ ✪ ✪ ✪
Security: ✪ ✪ ✪
Cleanliness: ✪ ✪ ✪ ✪ ✪

boundary for the Colville Indian Reservation. While there seems to be plenty of room for everyone to share in the lake's 80 acres of resources, the tribes have very specific regulations about fishing and hunting on their lands, so be as respectful of this as you would be of any private property owner if you plan to do some boating and/or fishing. Actually, you'll want to be more than respectful; the term is "law-abiding." They have the right to fine you. For the most part, a state fishing license is all you need if you stay in the middle of the lake, but if you happen to fish from the shore within the reservation, you need a reservation license. *Them's the rules.*

As a base camp for exploring all parts of the Okanogan highlands, lowlands, and benchlands in between, Crawfish Lake may not be the ideal choice. But then, the ideal choice won't have any camping spots available in the peak season! I've done my home-work and, in all honesty, you'll be hard-pressed to find anything comparable to Crawfish Lake. Especially for the price—*free*. When you weigh all the other factors, there is nothing in the entire Okanogan camping inventory that offers what Crawfish Lake has—(1) a great campsite, (2) a decent-sized lake, (3) easy access to the Okanogan's commercial zone (within 20 miles, all but the last couple of which are paved), (4) a rea-sonable altitude, (5) a highly scenic drive to and fro, (6) proximity to interesting byway and backway loops around Okanogan territory; and (7) the blessing that it is in the opposite direction to that where most of the camping crowd is headed.

Given that Crawfish Lake Campground's watery boundary backs up to a somewhat restrictive reserva-tion, any land-based activities you plan to pursue will be mostly north and west of here. This means either backtracking down FS 30 into the Tunk Valley (maybe stopping off at the Tunk Valley Wildlife Area) or stay-ing north on FS 30 (also known as Peterson Road as it leaves Tunk Valley) to connect with Aeneas Valley Road. I have not driven them, but along the way to Aeneas Valley, the Chewiliken Road threads its way through the Chewiliken Valley and appears to offer an interesting day-tripping route in the immediate vicinity

KEY INFORMATION

ADDRESS:	Crawfish Lake c/o Tonasket Ranger District 1 West Winesap Tonasket, WA 98855
OPERATED BY:	Okanogan National Forest
INFORMATION:	(509) 486-2186
OPEN:	April–October, weather permitting
SITES:	19
EACH SITE HAS:	Picnic table, fire pit with grill
ASSIGNMENT:	First come, first served
REGISTRATION:	Not necessary
FACILITIES:	Vault toilets; boat ramp; day-use area; no piped water; no garbage service
PARKING:	At individual site
FEE:	No fee
ELEVATION:	4,500 feet
RESTRICTIONS:	**Pets:** On leash **Fires:** In fire pits only **Alcohol:** Permitted **Vehicles:** Trailers and RVs up to 24 feet (tight turnarounds) **Other:** Southern half of lake is within the Colville Indian Reservation, where special fishing and hunting permits are required

MAP

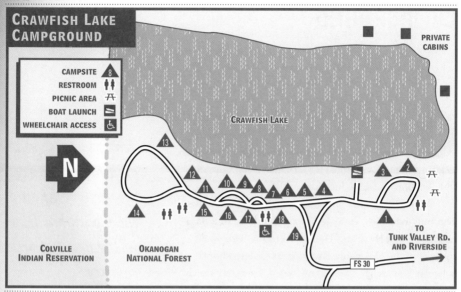

CRAWFISH LAKE CAMPGROUND

CAMPSITE	8
RESTROOM	
PICNIC AREA	
BOAT LAUNCH	
WHEELCHAIR ACCESS	

N

CRAWFISH LAKE

PRIVATE CABINS

13

12

11 10 9 8 7 6 5 4 3 2

14 15 16 17 18 1

19

COLVILLE INDIAN RESERVATION

OKANOGAN NATIONAL FOREST

FS 30

TO TUNK VALLEY RD. AND RIVERSIDE

GETTING THERE

From Riverside on US 97, go 18 miles east on County Road 9320 (Tunk Creek or Tunk Valley Road, depending on whom you ask), at which point the road becomes FS 30. Drive 2 miles, turn right onto spur 100, and the campground is less than a half mile on. Note: Despite what you may see on various road maps or what you may read otherwise, this is the best way to find Crawfish Lake. Trust me on this one.

of Crawfish Lake. The Chewiliken Road skirts around the base of Tunk Mountain, which has an access road to a lookout on top.

I haven't been able to get a satisfactory answer on the background of Crawfish Lake's namesake inhabitants. Maybe you can. Yet another reason to make Crawfish Lake your Okanogan base. When was the last time you had crawfish étouffée on the campstove?

DAROGA STATE PARK CAMPGROUND

OK, SO THE POWER LINES overhead may be a clue that you're not in the most wilderness-like setting in the state, but what Daroga State Park lacks in primitive environs, it more than makes up for with location, location, location.

What Daroga has going for it is the real estate it so flagrantly occupies, sprawled along the shore of a natural lagoon that separates Daroga from the wide main channel of the Columbia River on its eastern shore between Wenatchee and Lake Chelan. Formerly ranch and orchard lands owned by the Auvil family since the 1920s, the land was sold by son Grady to the state parks in 1981.

Thanks, Grady! You're a peach. And so was the signature strain of fruit produced in the orchard that first bore the name "Daroga," an awkward-sounding compilation of the Auvil boys' first names. Somehow, it stuck. Whatever prompted the sale of the 90 Auvil acres to the State of Washington is in itself about as fuzzy as a peach, but it seemed fitting to keep the name in honor of the local Auvil legacy.

The park is actually two distinct zones—the upland butte where the main campground with RVs, hookups, and general mayhem reign, and the lowly and lovely delta with serene riverfront, walk-in tent sites. The most you will have to contend with at the tent sites is a noisy boat motor or two, but it would be difficult for anyone but James Bond to make a serious intrusion with a mechanical contraption.

Parking for the walk-in sites is just south of the main park entrance. Park services conveniently include wheeled carts for carrying gear to the sites (all first come, first served) that are laid out in grassy splendor. With such open conditions, privacy is at a premium, but the trade-off is that there are no RVs, no lights in your face, no doors slamming in your ear, no genera-

> *Tent campers get their own broad, grassy meadow right on the Columbia River in the heart of orchard country.*

RATINGS

Beauty: ✰ ✰ ✰ ✰ ✰
Privacy: ✰
Spaciousness: ✰ ✰ ✰ ✰ ✰
Quiet: ✰ ✰ ✰
Security: ✰ ✰ ✰ ✰ ✰
Cleanliness: ✰ ✰ ✰ ✰ ✰

ADDRESS:	Daroga State Park One South Daroga Park Road Orondo, WA 98843
OPERATED BY:	Washington State Parks and Recreation Commission
INFORMATION:	(509) 664-6380
OPEN:	March 11– October 11
SITES:	17 walk-in/boat-in; 28 utility
EACH SITE HAS:	Picnic table, fire pit with grill
ASSIGNMENT:	First come, first served; group camps are reservable
REGISTRATION:	On site
FACILITIES:	Restrooms with showers; piped water; RV hookups; RV dump station; 2 group camps; picnic areas; wheelbarrows for transporting camping equipment to walk-in sites; pay telephone; firewood
PARKING:	Tent-camping parking separate on south side of complex; parking for utility sites at individual site
FEE:	$10 tent; $21 utility
ELEVATION:	800 feet
RESTRICTIONS:	Pets: On leash Fires: In fire pits only Alcohol: Permitted Vehicles: RVs and trailers of any length in utility sites

tors whining throughout the night. Just you, the river, the sky . . . and a few softly humming power lines.

Amenities at Daroga are in keeping with those at the more-developed state park facilities: restrooms with flush toilets, hot showers, conveniently placed water spigots, sturdy picnic tables, and deep-seated fire pits with grills. Park rangers seemed to be everywhere when I was there, so if you have any questions or needs, they are quick to help.

This side of the Columbia, a dramatic departure from the heavily forested mountain slopes to the west, is the stark beginnings of the "scablands," a terribly unglamorous geologic term that, simply put, identifies a dry canyon and the rimrock remains of glacial flow. In eastern Washington, this means moderately steep, relatively dusty, mostly rocky, intensely hot, and often windy—at least in the summertime. Down by the river, the cool current and the ever-present wind can be soothing relief, but take a short drive up US 2 to Waterville via Corbaley and Pine Canyons and feel the full blast of typical scabland conditions hit you as you crest the plateau.

For this reason, most activities around Daroga in the summertime tend to be water-oriented. The park has a great swimming area for a sultry summer morning plunge. Midday is siesta time. Nighttime is for stargazing and cowboy tunes around the campfire. If hiking is in your hot desert blood, the closest options are across the river in the Entiat Valley region (see Silver Falls entry, page 73) or north on the slopes above the Methow or Okanogan Valleys. Hiking the coulees of eastern Washington requires fortitude and an adequate water supply, but it can be done—and there is much geologic magic and mystery to behold—with the right preparation.

Not exactly a wilderness activity, but a growing revenue stream in the benchlands above the Columbia River, is golf. Several new highly touted courses built within the past several years are making headlines simply by their presence. This trend may signal a shift from dependency on the traditional agriculture-based economy that has permitted this region to thrive for many generations.

MAP

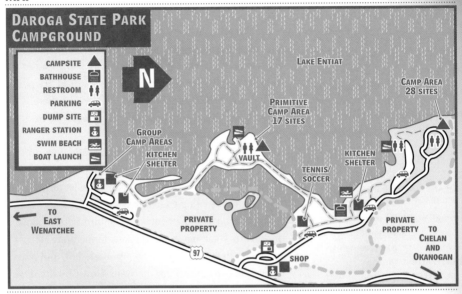

DAROGA STATE PARK CAMPGROUND

CAMPSITE	▲
BATHHOUSE	
RESTROOM	♀♂
PARKING	🚗
DUMP SITE	
RANGER STATION	
SWIM BEACH	
BOAT LAUNCH	

N

LAKE ENTIAT

CAMP AREA 28 SITES

PRIMITIVE CAMP AREA 17 SITES

GROUP CAMP AREAS

KITCHEN SHELTER

VAULT

KITCHEN SHELTER

TENNIS/ SOCCER

TO EAST WENATCHEE

PRIVATE PROPERTY

PRIVATE PROPERTY

TO CHELAN AND OKANOGAN

97

SHOP

Across the border, the Canadian Okanogan has been wildly successful in bringing visitors to its scenic splendors by combining award-winning wineries and world-class golf, and the Columbia benches are following suit. With an equally attractive climate and terrain, a host of grape growers and vintners have formed the Columbia Cascade Wine Group. If they have anything to do with it, the next measurable area of tourism growth in Washington State will be the "Columbia Highlands."

Get to Daroga as soon as you can.

GETTING THERE

From East Wenatchee, drive 18 miles north on US 97 (on the east side of the Columbia River). The park is on the left just past Orondo.

NORTH FORK NINE MILE CAMPGROUND

> *This is a delightfully spacious and forested encampment in a land once cherished by Native Americans and exploited by miners.*

NORTH FORK NINE MILE is to the western hills of the Okanogan Valley what Crawfish Lake is to the eastern plateau—a great base camp for exploring in just about every direction, whether by foot or by wheeled, motorized, or aquatic vehicle. In winter, strap on the cross-country skis or harness the malamute to the dogsled. This is an area as rich in Native American and white lore as it is in outdoor adventure. Combining the two is a perfect way to uncover the secret haunts and hideouts of those who have passed this way and perhaps create a few of your own.

Just down the road from Cold Springs (see page 122) but eminently more accessible, the North Fork Nine Mile camp—a delightfully spacious and wooded encampment within the boundaries of the Loomis State Forest—is also governed by the Department of Natural Resources and offers the same amazing value as Cold Springs (that is, it's free).

Although it doesn't have Cold Springs' views or mountaintop perch, North Fork Nine Mile (at a respectable 3,500 feet) does have hand-pumped water and high-bank real estate above North Fork Toats Coulee Creek. Go straight for site 5 and don't give it up—no matter how many gold nuggets or shots of whiskey someone may offer you. It's priceless! Of course, there is a slight drawback to site 5—found at the end of the loop drive, backing up to a steep embankment (to its right) and a creek down a steep embankment (to the left). There's not much room for error at site 5, so don't tell your enemies where you're headed, unless you have another escape route: the backdoor at site 5 is a mite tricky.

About a hundred years ago, everybody around Toats Coulee had at least one enemy, and this was evidenced in some pretty bizarre and grisly goings-on. The Sinlahekin were the small, local tribe who claimed

RATINGS

Beauty: ✪ ✪ ✪ ✪ ✪
Privacy: ✪ ✪ ✪ ✪ ✪
Spaciousness: ✪ ✪ ✪ ✪ ✪
Quiet: ✪ ✪ ✪ ✪
Security: ✪ ✪
Cleanliness: ✪ ✪ ✪

the lands of the narrow, namesake valley as their ancestral home. When gold was rumored to be plentiful "in them thar hills," every variety of white-faced opportunist descended on Loomis and the Sinlahekin, turning honest men into deranged schemers. Gold, silver, and copper were the main veins of luck pursued and, while no one got particularly rich, the Loomis area was a chaotic mix of swaggering miners, staggering Natives, and finagling merchants as everyone gave it their best shot. Add to this the herders of the Phelps & Wadleigh cattle station and you've got the ingredients for a tough-living town. Hard to imagine when you drive through this tiny, clapboarded outpost that it was once the largest metropolis in Okanogan County.

The Sinlahekins had as their dubious leader, Chief Sar-sarp-kin ("avalanche" in English), who boasted, boozed, and debauched his way around the Loomis and Toats Coulee lands in the last decades of the nineteenth century. Initially wary of the white man's intrusions, Chief Sar-sarp-kin came to be regarded as a mostly honorable Native whose only fault, probably, was loving his homeland—and liquor—too much. In the end, having prevailed in entreating the federal government to allow his people to remain in Toats Coulee (rather than be shipped off to the Colville Reservation across the Okanogan River), he was done in at the hands of his own son (or so it is believed) over a family property dispute. Indeed, a sadly ironic end to the colorful chief's life. But bad luck followed him even into modern times: a massive eight-foot marble monument, erected at his gravesite by the Indian Department in 1912 mysteriously disappeared between 1972 and 1988 and has never been recovered. Nor does it seem that anyone can recall exactly when, during that time, it went missing.

Other enigmatic ghosts of the upper Sinlahekin include most of Chief Sar-sarp-kin's immediate (and large) family, several boomtown-era newspaper editors, Guy Waring—one of the area's first merchants (who eventually made permanent quarters over in the Methow), and Julius Loomis—the rich eccentric who was the "official" founder of Loomiston (as it was first known) and who was reported to have gone mad.

KEY INFORMATION

ADDRESS: North Fork Nine Mile Campground c/o Northeast Region Office P.O. Box 190 225 South Silke Road Colville, WA 99114

OPERATED BY: Washington State Department of Natural Resources

INFORMATION: (509) 684-7474

OPEN: All year, weather permitting

SITES: 11

EACH SITE HAS: Picnic table, fire pit with grill

ASSIGNMENT: First come, first served

REGISTRATION: Not necessary

FACILITIES: Vault toilets; hand-pumped water; no garbage service

PARKING: At individual site

FEE: No fee

ELEVATION: 3,500 feet

RESTRICTIONS: Pets: On leash
Fires: In fire pits only
Alcohol: Permitted
Vehicles: Trailers and RVs up to 20 feet long
Other: Pack trash out

MAP

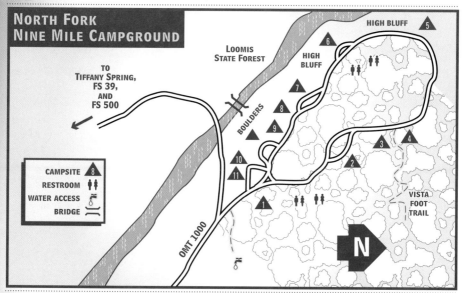

NORTH FORK NINE MILE CAMPGROUND

HIGH BLUFF 5

LOOMIS STATE FOREST

HIGH BLUFF

HIGH BLUFF 6

TO TIFFANY SPRING, FS 39, AND FS 500

7

BOULDERS

8

9

3

4

2

CAMPSITE 8
RESTROOM
WATER ACCESS
BRIDGE

10

11

VISTA FOOT TRAIL

1

OMT 1000

N

GETTING THERE

From Loomis, go north 2 miles on the Loomis–Oroville Road. Turn left on Toats Coulee Road and stay on OMT 1000, passing its junction with OMT 2000 (5.5 miles). Continue on OMT 1000 for another 2.5 miles to the campground, the entrance to which is found just before the road turns sharply up to the left, crossing over North Fork Toats Coulee Creek.

You'll go mad only trying to fit in all the fun things there are to do around Toats Coulee. Aside from stalking the history trail, you can enjoy the beautiful, high Chopaka Lake Basin and take the opportunity to go fly-fishing (the only fishing allowed). The road up to Chopaka can test you, presenting the same conditions that confronted the pioneers, so be prepared for rough and steep.

Deer hunters populate the fields and forests of the Sinlahekin in the fall, as is evidenced by the deer-skinning stations at North Fork Nine Mile campsites. Don't let this deter you from a foray up into the Pasayten Wilderness (where hunting is prohibited). The best access to Pasayten trails is at the Iron Gate trailhead on FS 500, which takes you quickly into broad meadows sweeping up to 8,000-foot peaks.

NORTHEASTERN WASHINGTON

FERRY LAKE CAMPGROUND

Republic

> *Where camping is for camping's sake . . . and maybe a little trout fishing and fossil finding, too!*

FOR THIS UPDATED AND expanded edition, I've chosen Ferry Lake over Swan Lake as the place to camp along the Sanpoil River drainage south of Republic. I visited these lakes in the summer of 2003, and it was quickly apparent to me that Swan Lake has become the gathering point for the crowds, such as they are, out here. If you're going to come all this way to a place where camping is pretty much camping-simply-for-the-sake-of-camping and you're like me, you want as much solitude as you can find. Ferry Lake and the even smaller Long Lake are much better choices than Swan. So far, there's no formal campground at the dainty, picture-perfect Fish Lake.

In this extreme southwestern corner of the 1.1-million-acre Colville National Forest, lakes are stocked with brooks and rainbows, which makes fishing the main draw, after the old-fashioned whiling away your time in serene, forested settings. At Ferry Lake, the nine campsites are lined up along the lake, and it often seems as if the fish want to help you out by practically throwing themselves into the frying pan—they surface that close to the lake's edge, seemingly undisturbed by human presence.

Fishing is best in early spring and fall. Down at Long Lake, "fly-fishing only" is the rule, and all motors (even electric, which are allowed on Ferry Lake) are verboten. Anyone fishing must have a Washington State fishing license, which can be purchased nearby in Republic. Kids under 15 don't need a license. Don't get caught fishing without a license or test the patience of the ranger by trying to pass as a 14-year-old.

If this means you end up in Republic for a license—and maybe a few camping supplies, too—make a point of visiting the Stonerose Interpretive Center adjacent to the Republic Historical Center. Not only can you view ancient, amazing fossilized impressions

RATINGS

Beauty: ✪ ✪ ✪ ✪
Privacy: ✪ ✪ ✪ ✪
Spaciousness: ✪ ✪ ✪ ✪ ✪
Quiet: ✪ ✪ ✪ ✪
Security: ✪ ✪ ✪
Cleanliness: ✪ ✪ ✪ ✪

THE BEST IN TENT CAMPING WASHINGTON
140

ADDRESS: Ferry Lake
Campground
c/o Republic Ranger
Station
P.O. Box 468
180 North Jefferson
Republic, WA 99166

OPERATED BY: Colville National
Forest

INFORMATION: (509) 775-7400

OPEN: April–October;
garbage collection
Memorial Day–
Labor Day

SITES: 9; site 9 can serve as
a group camp

EACH SITE HAS: Picnic table, fire pit
and grill; group site
has large fire pit and
3 benches

ASSIGNMENT: First come, first
served; no
reservations

REGISTRATION: Not necessary

FACILITIES: Vault toilets;
garbage pickup with
3 garbage contain-
ers; no piped water;
primitive boat ramp

PARKING: At individual sites

FEE: $6 per night; $2
extra vehicle

ELEVATION: 3,400 feet

RESTRICTIONS: **Pets:** On leash
Fires: In fire pits
only
Alcohol: Permitted
in campsite
Vehicles: RVs or
trailers up to 20 feet
Other: Fishing
license required; no
internal-combustion
boat engines on lake

of plants, insects, and fish that lived in the area together—and, apparently, nowhere else—nearly 50 million years ago, but for a fee, you can do your own digging and perhaps come home with your own Stonerose samples. The center allows people up to three fossils per person per day, but if you unearth something particularly noteworthy, they reserve the right to keep it. It's all in the name of scientific research. Maybe they'll name a rock after you, at least.

Evidence of previous activity around Ferry Lake is not quite as old as Stonerose fossils. The Civilian Conservation Corps hung around this territory back in the thirties and built, among many other structures, the one-of-a-kind kitchen shelter at Swan Lake that has become, intentionally or not, the epicenter of all campground activity. So if you've had your fill of too much isolated languishing over at Ferry Lake, take the trail between the two lakes (roughly 2 miles) and see what kind of action you can get in on at Swan—anything from an annual mountain biking festival to a private wedding (huckleberry canapé, anyone?) Technically part of the group site, which accommodates up to 50 people, it's mostly just shelter from inclement weather. This is why you're camped at Ferry.

Before the Civilian Conservation Corps showed up, Native Americans used many parts of the Colville forest's bountiful plant and berry harvests extensively for centuries. The campgrounds are essentially carved out of huckleberry patches shaded by larches, Douglas firs, and ponderosa pines. Veteran pickers have been returning to this area for decades, a tradition that is fostered by Republic forest managers who occasionally burn portions of the area's understory to regenerate the berry bushes.

Aside from fishing and berry-gathering, primary activities at Ferry Lake include hiking and mountain biking. The trail between Ferry and Swan Lakes can be extended to include the 2.2-mile loop around Swan Lake as well. On foot, it takes a good day to get there and back to camp, but you'll still have time to park yourself by the lake and settle in for the loon calls at twilight. Most fat-tire enthusiasts will prefer to seek out more demanding routes, and there are 50 miles of them

MAP

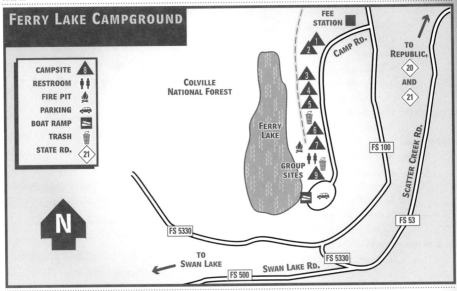

FERRY LAKE CAMPGROUND

CAMPSITE **8**
RESTROOM
FIRE PIT
PARKING
BOAT RAMP
TRASH
STATE RD. **21**

COLVILLE NATIONAL FOREST

FEE STATION

CAMP RD.

TO REPUBLIC, AND **20** **21**

FERRY LAKE

GROUP SITES

FS 100

SCATTER CREEK RD.

FS 53

N

FS 5330

TO SWAN LAKE

FS 500

SWAN LAKE RD.

FS 5330

starting to appear on logging routes closed to motor vehicles. Popular routes go past beaver ponds—where the occasional moose can be found, and along Sheep Mountain and its views of the Kettle River Range.

Cool, wet weather prevails at Ferry Lake in the spring, whereas temperatures are generally very pleasant in the seventies or eighties in summer. Bugs are surprisingly not an issue here, and that could easily be the main reason you decide to seek out this relatively undiscovered part of Washington State. Mosquitoes can be pesky in early summer, but with the kinds of summers we've had lately, their presence will be short-lived. A common annoyance elsewhere, biting flies are rarely a problem here.

GETTING THERE

From Republic on WA 20, drive 8.5 miles south on WA 21 along the Sanpoil River. Turn west on Scatter Creek Road (FS 53). Follow this paved road 6 miles. Turn north (right) on FS 5330 and go 1 mile, then head north again on FS 100 to the lake and campground.

HAAG COVE CAMPGROUND

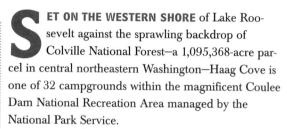

> *A 130-mile-long lake, mountains with the highest pass in Washington, an abundant diversity of wildlife, and the rich cultural heritage of a Native American nation nearby.*

SET ON THE WESTERN SHORE of Lake Roosevelt against the sprawling backdrop of Colville National Forest—a 1,095,368-acre parcel in central northeastern Washington—Haag Cove is one of 32 campgrounds within the magnificent Coulee Dam National Recreation Area managed by the National Park Service.

Despite its proximity to Kettle Falls, the campground does not seem overrun and besieged the way so many of the other campgrounds in the recreation area are. The fact that it has no boat launch may be one of the reasons that it gets less attention, because boating—mostly fast, mostly noisy—is a primary pastime of those who play within the recreation area.

I like it a lot for that reason. Plus, it's a very pretty and minimalist spot. The sites are well spaced, all have views of the lake and hillsides to the east, and there aren't enough of them to give one a sense of crowdedness. The best sites are on the south side (4 through 7) being large and close to the lake, and having their own parking space. These will be grabbed by the RVers first, but don't feel obliged to leave them empty if you get first choice. Sites 10 through 18 are mainly walk-ins with a common parking area, but they are configured more intimately. So, for maximum privacy, try for those closest to the lake. Leave the ones on the loop for latecomers who are happy to get a space at all.

The irony of Haag Cove's exquisite setting amid towering ponderosa pine and Douglas fir is that its existence depends on a purely man-made landmark. Lake Roosevelt is actually formed by the Columbia River. It was created when the monolithic Grand Coulee Dam was built in 1941 to harness the free-flowing power of the Columbia.

While you won't find the hundreds of salmon that used to attract Native Americans to Kettle Falls, there

RATINGS

Beauty: ✿ ✿ ✿ ✿ ✿
Privacy: ✿ ✿ ✿ ✿
Spaciousness: ✿ ✿ ✿ ✿ ✿
Quiet: ✿ ✿ ✿ ✿ ✿
Security: ✿ ✿ ✿
Cleanliness: ✿ ✿ ✿ ✿

are 30 other species of game fish that make Lake Roosevelt a popular angling destination. You'll need a Washington State license, which you can pick up at area marinas or hardware and sporting goods stores. If you are unfamiliar with the territory, you may want to stop at the visitor center in Kettle Falls for informative brochures and maps. Boats of every shape and size, motorized and unmotorized, ply the waters of Lake Roosevelt. With 660 miles of shoreline, there's plenty of room for everyone. But if you plan to do some boating, be advised of the dos and don'ts on this particular body of water. Lake level varies according to season. It is lowered as much as 100 feet in the wintertime, but walking the lake's exposed shoreline can make for an interesting outing on land.

Despite humankind's capricious rendering of the region's contours, this rugged, barren landscape gives one the sense of being an unspoiled environment. Deep canyons, sagebrush hills, and forested mountains are home to many varieties of animal and bird populations. One of the best spots for observing and shooting (with a camera) is just north of Haag Cove in Sherman Creek Habitat Management Area. Besides being a pretty area to explore, these 8,000 acres are safeguarded by the Washington Department of Game, which protects the deer's winter habitat and the habitat of other mammals all year.

The confluence of Sherman Creek and Lake Roosevelt produces a quality fly-fishing spot. The only other campground in the vicinity is Sherman Creek. However, it is one of the few campgrounds in eastern Washington that is accessible only by boat.

Hiking options are plentiful and relatively uncrowded in Colville National Forest. A gentler terrain, drier climate, and longer season compared to the Cascade area make for ideal backcountry conditions here. Sherman Pass, to the west on WA 20, is the high-altitude start (5,575 feet) for trails north and south into the Kettle River Range. Across Lake Roosevelt to the east is Huckleberry Range. Check with the Kettle Falls Ranger District for trail information.

Generally, the climate is warm and dry in summer months, with daytime temperatures ranging between

KEY INFORMATION

ADDRESS:	Haag Cove Campground c/o National Park Service 1368 South Kettle Park Road Kettle Falls, WA 99141
OPERATED BY:	National Park Service
INFORMATION:	(509) 738-6366; www.nps.gov/laro
OPEN:	All year
SITES:	18
EACH SITE HAS:	Picnic table, fire grill
ASSIGNMENT:	First come, first served; no reservations
REGISTRATION:	Not necessary
FACILITIES:	Piped water; pit toilets; boat dock; no boat launch
PARKING:	At individual sites
FEE:	$10 per night, May–October only; $5 during winter
ELEVATION:	2,500 feet
RESTRICTIONS:	**Pets:** On leash **Fires:** In fire pits only **Alcohol:** Permitted in campsite **Vehicles:** RVs or trailers up to 26 feet **Other:** Fishing license required; boat launch permit required; 7-day permit $6, 1-year permit $30 before May 1, $40 after

MAP

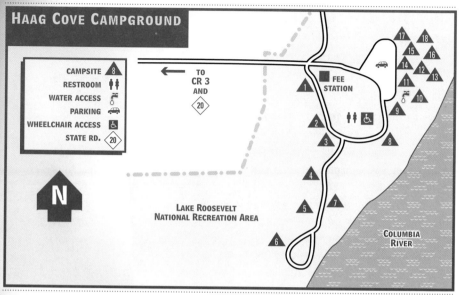

HAAG COVE CAMPGROUND

CAMPSITE   8
RESTROOM
WATER ACCESS
PARKING
WHEELCHAIR ACCESS
STATE RD.   20

TO CR 3 AND   20

N

FEE STATION

LAKE ROOSEVELT
NATIONAL RECREATION AREA

COLUMBIA RIVER

GETTING THERE

From Kettle Falls (81 miles northwest of Spokane), drive west on WA 20 across the upper portion of the Columbia River. Stay on WA 20 as it turns south along the river to the turnoff for Inchelium–Kettle Falls Road (CR 3) at about 7 miles. Take Inchelium–Kettle Falls Road south 5 miles to the campground.

75 °F and 100 °F. Temperatures drop to between 50 °F and 60 °F at night. Spring and fall are cooler but still dry and very pleasant. Eastern Washington winters vary but can often be cold and snowy. Since Haag Cove is open all year, check current weather conditions if you plan an off-season outing. Remember, Sherman Pass is the highest in the state and may prove impassable in bad weather.

A number of self-guided driving tours and scenic routes not far from Haag Cove offer another perspective of Coulee Dam country. Bangs Mountain Loop, for example, takes you through stands of old-growth ponderosa pine. Historical points of interest at Fort Spokane and in Kettle Falls can be combined with a lovely drive on WA 25, which parallels Lake Roosevelt on the east side.

LITTLE PEND OREILLE NATIONAL WILDLIFE REFUGE CAMPGROUNDS

LET'S GET THIS OUT of the way. "Pond Oray." If you already know how to pronounce this unusual, French-sounding Indian name, you're either a Washington native or you've lived here at least a decade.

But if you've never been here, native or not, you are missing one of the supreme treasures of this state. A true safari, Washington State–style.

From the populated west side of the Cascades, the refuge should not be considered unless you have a full week to devote to getting there and being there. Just southeast of Colville and less than two hours north of Spokane, Little Pend Oreille National Wildlife Refuge (LPONWR from here on out) is a 40,200-acre tract on the western slope of the Selkirk Mountains and easily a good day's drive from Seattle. It has the distinction of being the only mountainous, mixed-conifer preserve in the United States (not including Alaska), with six distinct forest zones, unquestionably worthy of the drive but most enjoyable with a little advance planning.

And that is just the beginning of the superlatives describing this sanctuary, remarkable not only for the ongoing wildlife preservation and restoration efforts but also for the aura of serenity that seems to settle on you like a comforting blanket almost as soon as you arrive. It's a place where you find yourself whispering a lot and feeling guilty about the automobile noise. Driving faster than 10 miles per hour seems reckless. It induces a kind of reverence, in essence, with a bit of breathless anticipation thrown in.

The campgrounds of the LPONWR are situated along what is termed the "Wildlife Viewing Route" on the refuge map. All are primitive, with fire rings, but they serve the purpose and do not intrude unnecessarily into the tranquil landscape. Designated dispersed campsites are sprinkled throughout the refuge and are mainly

> *If you can pronounce this one properly, you have lived in Washington for at least ten years. But if you haven't been here yet, you're missing a state treasure!*

RATINGS

Beauty: ✩ ✩ ✩ ✩ ✩
Privacy: ✩ ✩ ✩ ✩
Spaciousness: ✩ ✩ ✩ ✩
Quiet: ✩ ✩ ✩ ✩
Security: ✩ ✩ ✩
Cleanliness: ✩ ✩ ✩ ✩ ✩

ADDRESS: Little Pend Oreille
National Wildlife
Refuge
1310 Bear Creek
Road
Colville, WA 99114

OPERATED BY: U.S. Fish & Wildlife
Service

INFORMATION: (509) 684-8384

OPEN: April 14–December
31; designated
dispersed camping
October 1–
December 1

SITES: 4 established campgrounds with multi-
ple camp sites;
various designated
dispersed sites
throughout refuge

EACH SITE HAS: Picnic table, metal
fire ring with grill

ASSIGNMENT: First come, first
served

REGISTRATION: Not necessary

FACILITIES: Pit toilets; fishing
platforms; wildlife-
viewing areas; no
potable water on the
refuge

PARKING: At established campgrounds and at indi-
vidual dispersed
sites

FEE: No fee

ELEVATION: Ranges from 1,800 to
5,610 feet

RESTRICTIONS: Pets: Dogs on leash
at all times
Fires: In fire rings
only; use downed
wood only for camp-
fires
Alcohol: Permitted
Vehicles: On estab-
lished roads only;
ORV use prohibited;
mountain bikes on
maintained roads
and trails only

for hunters in the fall; they are available from October 1 through December 31. Recent changes have been introduced regarding camping, and I have a feeling that my favorite site under the big tree at Potter's Pond may not be as accessible as it once was. Disappointing, to be sure, but one must abide by the adjustments that the U.S. Fish & Wildlife Service makes to protect the natural landscape—the reason we're here in the first place.

Protecting such areas was what motivated the early conservation movement that President Franklin Roosevelt supported when he signed the refuge into existence in 1939. Roosevelt created a total of 535 refuges, all so designated expressly to preserve vital wildlife habitats around the country. In the case of LPONWR, the purpose was to provide breeding grounds for migratory birds. Since its designation, the LPONWR has become an important management facility for an assortment of other wildlife as well.

Before it got protected status, the LPONWR hosted a variety of people who found compelling reasons of their own to inhabit the lands of the Little Pend Oreille. The first, of course, were transient Native Americans who used trails through the Little Pend Oreille Valley to reach the rich camas fields farther east and to socialize with other tribes at gathering points in the interior.

White man's exploration of the area was initiated by Canada's North West Company in the early 1800s not long after Lewis and Clark made their historic expedition west. Today the refuge still retains evidence of homesteading, logging, and mining activity that occurred around the turn of the century. Some of the established campgrounds are the sites of former logging camps.

As you might imagine, birds are the focal point around the refuge. More than 180 species have been identified—from the regal bald eagle, who winters on the Little Pend Oreille River, to the warbling vireo, who makes its summer home on the refuge but flies south to Central America for the winter. The refuge maintains a checklist of birds known or anticipated to spend time there in any given season.

Bird-watching is followed in popularity by fishing.

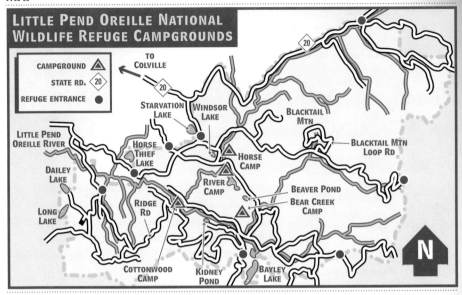

LITTLE PEND OREILLE NATIONAL WILDLIFE REFUGE CAMPGROUNDS

CAMPGROUND △
STATE RD. ⟨20⟩
REFUGE ENTRANCE ●

TO COLVILLE
20
STARVATION LAKE
WINDSOR LAKE
BLACKTAIL MTN
LITTLE PEND OREILLE RIVER
HORSE THIEF LAKE
BLACKTAIL MTN LOOP RD
DAILEY LAKE
HORSE CAMP
RIVER CAMP
BEAVER POND
BEAR CREEK CAMP
LONG LAKE
RIDGE RD
COTTONWOOD CAMP
KIDNEY POND
BAYLEY LAKE
N

The refuge has three lakes, the Little Pend Oreille River, numerous tributaries, and an assortment of beaver ponds that are open to those casting a line for catchable or catch-and-release fish throughout the fishing season. Two of the lakes are for fly-fishing only.

Wildlife viewing ranks at the top of my personal list of reasons to camp at LPONWR, and as I write this entry, I am mentally planning my trip back there soon. My only dilemma is choosing the best season. Spring lets loose the delightful songbirds and brings out the bears, and summer shows off colorful hummingbirds, the painted turtle, red-tailed hawks, and wild turkeys. Fall gets into hunting season, a good time to stay away. Winter will find me camping at the nearest Colville motel but offers snowy perspectives on the snowshoe hare, pygmy owl, stealthy cougars, and furtive bobcats.

It's a tough call. I suppose I'll just have to "pond oray" that one for a while. . .

GETTING THERE

From Colville, drive 6 miles east on WA 20. Turn right onto Artman–Gibson Road. At 1.7 miles (a four-way intersection), turn left onto Kitt–Narcisse Road and follow it 2.2 miles to the end of the pavement and a fork with two dirt roads. Bear right onto Bear Creek Road. The refuge headquarters is 3.3 miles down. There is an information kiosk at the entrance to the headquarters.

LYMAN LAKE CAMPGROUND

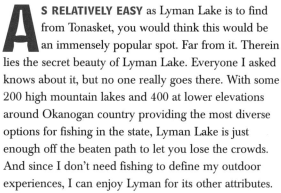

> *If you want small, secluded, and serene, you get it all in a ponderosa pine forest in the remote southeastern corner of the Okanogan National Forest.*

AS RELATIVELY EASY as Lyman Lake is to find from Tonasket, you would think this would be an immensely popular spot. Far from it. Therein lies the secret beauty of Lyman Lake. Everyone I asked knows about it, but no one really goes there. With some 200 high mountain lakes and 400 at lower elevations around Okanogan country providing the most diverse options for fishing in the state, Lyman Lake is just enough off the beaten path to let you lose the crowds. And since I don't need fishing to define my outdoor experiences, I can enjoy Lyman for its other attributes.

Lyman Lake was truly off the beaten path for me—I got to it in a backdoor kind of way, relying on dumb luck, actually. I was on an extended road research trip in the summer of 2003 and had already covered several hundred miles of the central Columbia River Basin by making a huge loop, starting in Lake Chelan on the morning of the first day and returning there on the night of the second. Don't try this if you are out to have a relaxing time or need your car to last several more years.

At any rate, after a delightful breeze through the Ferry Lake group (see page 140), I was all for a shortcut to my next destination. Checked the map. Looked simple enough. West Sanpoil River Road. Well, I'm here to tell you that there is no "official" West Sanpoil Road, just a goat track that masquerades as a Forest Service road on most maps. (You'll come to learn that this is common out here in the wilds of the Okanogan National Forest.)

Applying my best bushwhacking skills (in a car), I forged ahead, flattening old-growth weeds in my path (remorselessly), juddering across more cattle guards than I could count (methinks I have passed over a few too many to be going in the right direction), and crossing streambeds that didn't appear to have been disturbed

RATINGS

Beauty: ☆ ☆ ☆ ☆ ☆
Privacy: ☆ ☆ ☆ ☆
Spaciousness: ☆ ☆ ☆ ☆
Quiet: ☆ ☆ ☆ ☆
Security: ☆ ☆ ☆
Cleanliness: ☆ ☆ ☆ ☆ ☆

since the last fur trappers skulked through. My perseverance and gut instinct paid off, and within several hours I burst out onto the edge of the beautiful Aeneas Valley. From there, I followed the signs to Lyman Lake.

When I pulled in, a Forest Service ranger was just arriving as well. This I took as a very good sign. Although I was on the outer fringes of Forest Service jurisdiction and at the last public stop before venturing into the private reserve of the Colville Nation down the Lyman Lake–Moses Meadows Road, I found that Lyman was not outside Forest Service supervision radar after all.

However, there's not a whole lot to supervise. Lyman is only four sites with picnic tables, fire rings, and grills. One pit toilet. A no-frills kind of place. A dispersed camping area for hunters is around the far side of the lake, and a semblance of a boat launch (for hand-carried, nonmotorized boats only) is on the southern end.

Lyman is small only in the number of campsites, however, and I'm kind of glad that the Forest Service has not seen the need to add more. There is certainly plenty of room to do so. A long access road reveals much undeveloped land on either side, and the same goes for most of the area in the campground proper that is not a camping site per se. This makes for sites that are defined not by their proximity to each other but rather by how much space you feel you need to establish your claim. Each of the sites sits with at least one boundary on Lyman Lake. The lake itself only takes up four acres, so the general sense (if you are not having to share with others) is that you've stumbled on a delightfully private little oasis.

If, like me, you're not much for fishing, the area around Lyman Lake is laced with trails that take you to high points above the valley floor for superb views. The Aeneas Valley makes for a great driving tour, with an "Old West" feeling represented in the ranch buildings dotting the broad pasturelands. A good loop trip for sampling the local terrain would combine Cape LaBelle Road, WA 20, and Aeneas Valley Road.

KEY INFORMATION

ADDRESS:	Lyman Lake c/o Tonasket Ranger District 1 West Winesap Tonasket, WA 98855
OPERATED BY:	Okanogan National Forest
INFORMATION:	(509) 486-2186
OPEN:	Late April–October, weather permitting
SITES:	4
EACH SITE HAS:	Picnic table, fire pit with grill
ASSIGNMENT:	First come, first served
REGISTRATION:	On site
FACILITIES:	Vault toilet; no piped water; no garbage service
PARKING:	At individual site
FEE:	No fee
ELEVATION:	2,900 feet
RESTRICTIONS:	**Pets:** On leash **Fires:** In fire pits only **Alcohol:** Permitted **Vehicles:** Trailers and RVs up to 24 feet

MAP

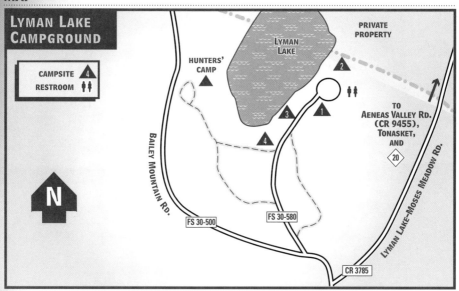

LYMAN LAKE CAMPGROUND

CAMPSITE **4**
RESTROOM

HUNTERS' CAMP

LYMAN LAKE

PRIVATE PROPERTY

2

3 **1**

4

BAILEY MOUNTAIN RD.

FS 30-500

FS 30-580

N

TO AENEAS VALLEY RD. (CR 9455), TONASKET, AND

20

LYMAN LAKE-MOSES MEADOW RD.

CR 3785

GETTING THERE

From Tonasket, go 18 miles east on WA 20 to CR 9455 (Aeneas Valley Road). Turn right and drive 13 miles to CR 3785 (Lyman Lake– Moses Meadow Road). Turn right, and you'll see the campground 2.5 miles in on the right.

By the way, if you *do* fancy fishing at Lyman Lake, it's stocked with Eastern Brook, and I hear it's fantastic in the fall. But keep that to yourself.

SOUTHEASTERN WASHINGTON

BROOKS MEMORIAL STATE PARK CAMPGROUND

IN THE EARLY DAYS of my short-lived career as a river-rafting guide, I was part of the historic first commercial descent of the Klickitat River, a small, lively, and rapidly dropping tumble of water that courses off the slopes of Gilbert Peak high in the Goat Rocks Wilderness. Plunging south through the basalt-lined canyons of the Yakama Indian Reservation east of Mount Adams, the Klickitat finally succumbs to anonymity as it empties into the Columbia River at the small town of Lyle.

It was my dubious luck to hang around with a rag-tag group of egocentric boaters who were always seeking the aquatic version of "steep and deep." You skiers know what I mean.

The Klickitat fit the bill—steep and narrow descents, nightmarish S-curves, and boulders and logs everywhere. To make a long story short, the river won. Klickitat: 2, ragtag humiliated group of boaters: 0.

Fortunately you'll find more than just hair-raising river running to keep you busy if you're in the Goldendale area and need a campground for the night. From its 3,000-foot location in the Simcoe Mountains, Brooks Memorial State Park is a good base for exploring not only the Klickitat Valley but also sights farther south toward the Columbia River, west into the untamed Klickitat River region and to Mount Adams, and north along the Yakama Indian Reservation and into the viticultural lands of the Yakima Valley.

There are many points of interest in all directions. Central to the area is Goldendale, a quiet community that is home to the Goldendale Observatory State Park Interpretive Center and one of the largest telescopes open to the public in the country.

Down along the Columbia, historical attractions include Maryhill Museum and the American version of Stonehenge. Maryhill Museum houses the world-

> *Situated at roughly 3,000 feet in the Simcoe Mountains, Brooks Memorial makes for an excellent by-the-highway base camp for exploring the lovely scenery of the Klickitat Valley.*

RATINGS

Beauty: ✿ ✿ ✿
Privacy: ✿ ✿ ✿
Spaciousness: ✿ ✿ ✿
Quiet: ✿ ✿ ✿ ✿ ✿
Security: ✿ ✿ ✿ ✿
Cleanliness: ✿ ✿ ✿ ✿ ✿

KEY INFORMATION

ADDRESS: Brooks Memorial State Park
2465 US 97
Goldendale, WA 98620

OPERATED BY: Washington State Parks and Recreation Commission

INFORMATION: (509) 773-4611

OPEN: All year; limited winter facilities November–March

SITES: 22 standard; 23 utility

EACH SITE HAS: Picnic table, fire grill

SOME SITES: Water and hookups for RVs

ASSIGNMENT: First come, first served; no reservations

REGISTRATION: Self-registration

FACILITIES: Restrooms with flush toilets, sinks, hot showers; 2 kitchen shelters with picnic tables, sinks, electricity; public telephone; playground; primitive group camp; Environmental Learning Center for up to 104 people; firewood for sale; store within 1 mile

PARKING: At campground and at individual sites

FEE: $15 standard per night; $21 hookup; $10 each additional vehicle

ELEVATION: Nearly 3,000 feet

RESTRICTIONS: Pets: On leash
Fires: In fire pits; no firewood gathering
Alcohol: Permitted at campsite or picnic site
Vehicles: RVs up to 40 feet

famous art collection of Sam—Who-in-the-Sam-Hill—Hill and his wife, Mary. Also the brainchild of Hill, the Stonehenge Memorial, which copies its English namesake in size, honors Klickitat County's young men who fought and died in World War I.

The entire area around Goldendale had an eventful past. The Klickitat Indian tribe has inhabited the region for hundreds of years and was instrumental in negotiating between eastern and western tribes who gathered in the region to trade and socialize. At Horsethief Lake State Park (on WA 14 along the Columbia), you can see Indian petroglyphs.

This is the dry side of the Cascades, which means hot and dry summers with cool nights. Winters are generally chilly and snowy. Brooks Memorial is open year-round and offers seasonal activities. Summer and fall are best for enjoying the 9 miles of hiking trails that follow the Little Klickitat River up into meadows for sensational up-close views of Mount Hood. Winter offers cross-country skiing, snowmobiling, and snowshoeing. Wildflowers bloom prolifically in the park from March until July, and there is quite a diversity of park wildlife at various times of the year—turkey, deer, raccoon, porcupine, beaver, bobcat, coyote, red-tailed hawk, and owl. The Little Klickitat River follows US 97 from Brooks Memorial down into Goldendale, and it is not uncommon to observe beavers going about their business of damming the river. Additional activities around Goldendale include golfing, windsurfing on the Columbia at Doug's Beach State Park, bicycling, and rock climbing.

Despite my tale of woe at the beginning of this chapter, river running is also an enjoyable option. Both the Klickitat and the White Salmon offer their share of thrills and chills. The characteristics of both rivers make them best suited to kayak descents, but our pioneering rafting effort has contributed to the popularity of rafting as well. Check out the local guide services for more information on this.

Your choice of campsite at Brooks Memorial will be based on what's available on their first-come, first-served system. If it's a weekday, off-season, or winter, you'll get your pick of spacious sites. Go for the ones

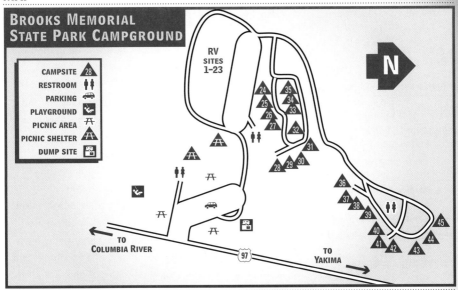

farthest from the road, which are, fortunately, tent sites 24 through 45 (although it's a lonely place, and at night cars are few). I noticed that some of the tent sites are a bit awkwardly positioned up the hillside, so finding a level spot for the tent can be a challenge. Foliage is thin between sites, too, so finding privacy can also be a trial. The higher up the hillside you go, the more privacy and the more slope, so weigh your priorities accordingly.

GETTING THERE

From Yakima, follow US 97 south for 55 miles, crossing Satus Pass (elevation 3,107 feet) to the park entrance on the right. Administrative and maintenance buildings and the Environmental Learning Center are across US 97 on the left.

FIELDS SPRING STATE PARK CAMPGROUND

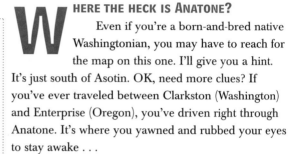

> *This park is a handy wilderness escape from Clarkston and Lewiston, an ideal layover between destinations north and south, or a destination of its own.*

WHERE THE HECK IS ANATONE?

WEven if you're a born-and-bred native Washingtonian, you may have to reach for the map on this one. I'll give you a hint. It's just south of Asotin. OK, need more clues? If you've ever traveled between Clarkston (Washington) and Enterprise (Oregon), you've driven right through Anatone. It's where you yawned and rubbed your eyes to stay awake . . .

Needless to say, Anatone is quite small—but significant in the world of tent camping. It is the last stop for any kind of services before one continues on to Fields Spring State Park. That means that anything you need that they didn't have in Anatone is all the way back in Clarkston or Lewiston (Idaho). Beyond Fields Spring to the south lies wilderness, national forest, and wild river canyons. Maybe you better make one last review of that checklist.

Literally on the edge of nowhere (which is where most tent campers like to find themselves), Fields Spring State Park is actually a handy wilderness escape for folks from Clarkston and Lewiston (both about 20 miles away). For anyone else, the park is an ideal layover between destinations north and south or can be a destination of its own. From the urban centers of western Washington and Oregon, it is easily an eight-hour drive. Admittedly, it is well off the beaten path, but that is part of its appeal. Besides, the roads are good all the way there. When the next long holiday weekend comes up, here's one to consider.

Sitting on a basalt foundation at 4,000 feet on the eastern edge of Washington's Blue Mountains, Fields Spring State Park is open all year and hosts activities in every season. It is a place of unusual beauty in an otherwise harsh and rugged terrain, created by one of the largest and deepest lava flows in the world's geologic

RATINGS

Beauty: ✿ ✿ ✿ ✿ ✿
Privacy: ✿ ✿ ✿
Spaciousness: ✿ ✿ ✿ ✿ ✿
Quiet: ✿ ✿ ✿ ✿
Security: ✿ ✿ ✿ ✿
Cleanliness: ✿ ✿ ✿ ✿ ✿

history. Evidence of this massive, recurring lava activity, known as the Columbia Plateau, can best be seen in the walls of river gorges and canyons throughout southeastern Washington.

One of the best places to view the canyons themselves is right at the state park. Unless you've brought your hangglider or parasail (an increasingly popular way to tour the area), a 1-mile hike up 4,500-foot Puffer Butte (elevation gain: 500 feet) provides vistas into both the Grande Ronde River and the mighty Snake River canyons and across Washington, Oregon, and Idaho, whose borders converge in this corner. While the Snake River is practically a household name, with its immensely popular boating adventures, the Grande Ronde is relatively obscure, wandering northeast from Oregon's Anthony Lakes region (see *The Best in Tent Camping: Oregon* if you're continuing on in that direction). Of its total 185 miles, the Washington stretch of the Grande Ronde is mostly a drift trip with Class II and III rapids. It is not considered a highly technical river, but deceptively powerful eddies during high water and rocks at low periods require you to be experienced.

Paddlers looking for greater technical challenges should venture upstream into the Oregon sector. Parts of the river's Oregon flow are designated wild and scenic, and there are several put-in spots not far from Fields Spring. Take a good road map of the area if you plan to do any shuttling.

Escaping the heat of the summer is one of the biggest draws to Fields Spring. Although the 792 park acres sit on what is essentially an arid, desert-like plateau with prickly pear cactus growing down along the Grande Ronde's banks, the difference in elevation makes all the difference in temperature. While Clarkston and Lewiston swelter in 100 °F agony in midsummer, Fields Spring rarely gets above a tolerable 85 °F.

However, winter is a different story. Snowy conditions make for ideal cross-country ski outings, and the park staff maintains approximately 8 miles of trails.

In springtime, catch the spectacular wildflower display or see if you can identify all eight species of woodpeckers that nest in and among the stands of

KEY INFORMATION

ADDRESS: Fields Spring State Park P.O. Box 37 Anatone, WA 99401

OPERATED BY: Washington State Parks and Recreation Commission

INFORMATION: (509) 256-3332

OPEN: All year, snow permitting

SITES: 20

EACH SITE HAS: Picnic table, fire pit with grill, shade trees

ASSIGNMENT: First come, first served; no reservations

REGISTRATION: Self-registration on site

FACILITIES: Bathhouse with sinks, toilets, showers (25 cents), hot water; kitchen shelter with electricity; wood stove; public telephone; firewood (in lodges only); playground; limited disabled access; Environmental Learning Center with 2 lodges for group rental; restaurant and ice nearby

PARKING: At individual sites

FEE: $15 per night standard site; $5 per night primitive site

ELEVATION: 4,000 feet

RESTRICTIONS: Pets: On leash
Fires: In fire pits only
Alcohol: Permitted
Vehicles: No hookups for RVs or trailers

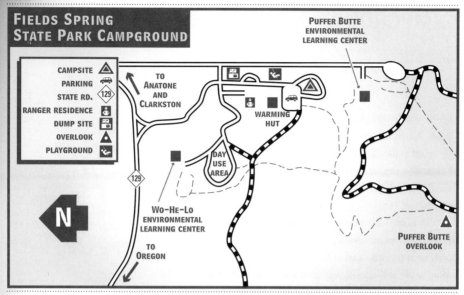

FIELDS SPRING STATE PARK CAMPGROUND

PUFFER BUTTE ENVIRONMENTAL LEARNING CENTER

CAMPSITE
PARKING
STATE RD.
RANGER RESIDENCE
DUMP SITE
OVERLOOK
PLAYGROUND

TO ANATONE AND CLARKSTON

WARMING HUT

DAY USE AREA

WO-HE-LO ENVIRONMENTAL LEARNING CENTER

TO OREGON

PUFFER BUTTE OVERLOOK

GETTING THERE

From Clarkston (roughly 110 miles south of Spokane), follow WA 129 south through Asotin for 21 miles and then head 4 miles past Anatone to the park entrance.

western larch, grand fir, Douglas fir, and ponderosa pine that shade the campsites.

The campground itself is a simple affair with 20 tent spaces that double as RV sites without hookups. There is no bad spot among the 20 unless you've got an inconsiderate neighbor. For a state park this small, it is indeed a treat to have restrooms with showers, so take advantage.

Whether you're passing through or making this corner of Washington the destination, Fields Spring is a true tent camper's oasis in a region otherwise parched for camping options.

GODMAN CAMPGROUND

FOR THOSE OF YOU looking for an ends-of-the-Earth destination complete with (gulp!) stories of stalking mountain lions, read on. For those of you who prefer to find your own adventures rather than having them find you, look up Tucannon (see entry, page 166).

Godman Campground is the sacred domain of modern-day explorers who have a healthy appetite for bone-jarring roads and cliff-hanging vistas, and an unflappable self-confidence in the face of some really badly marked Forest Service roads (or maybe it was just my map). At any rate, I think it's highly probable that even the intrepid Lewis and Clark found themselves scratching their heads up here.

Presto! A campground name was born!

If Tucannon, at a mere 2,600-foot elevation, is the last bastion of civilized camping adventure in the Umatilla, then Godman—at 6,050 feet—is the start of all things wild . . . beginning with stories we heard from a couple cruising through as part of an anniversary-weekend celebration. OK, that's not the wild part! Calamity Jane meets Davy Crockett, you may think. Actually, they couldn't have looked more suburban in their minivan and gawky white tennis shoes. Suddenly, I didn't feel very remote.

Turns out they had it on good authority that the mountain lion threat around Godman can be very real. We all shot quick glances around as we stood very obviously in the wide open spaces of the Forest Service road, one eye on the tree limbs above. We talked louder than we needed to. We laughed nervously. Suddenly, I felt remote as hell.

Well, as the Umatilla Forest Service advises you on their Web site, spending time in the wilderness involves an "element of risk." This caveat aside, the Wenaha–Tucannon Wilderness is too splendid of an outback

Perhaps named when Meriwether said to William, "God, man, where in blazes are we?"

RATINGS

Beauty: ✪ ✪ ✪ ✪ ✪
Privacy: ✪ ✪ ✪
Spaciousness: ✪ ✪ ✪ ✪ ✪
Quiet: ✪ ✪ ✪ ✪ ✪
Security: ✪ ✪ ✪
Cleanliness: ✪ ✪ ✪ ✪ ✪

ADDRESS: Godman
Campground
c/o Pomeroy Ranger
District
71 West Main
Pomeroy, WA 99347

OPERATED BY: Umatilla National
Forest

INFORMATION: (509) 843-1891; also
cabin and lookout
reservations

OPEN: Camping mid-June–
late October; cabin
available all year

SITES: 8

EACH SITE HAS: Picnic table, fire pit
with grill

ASSIGNMENT: First come, first
served

REGISTRATION: Not necessary for
camping; reserva-
tions for cabin rental

FACILITIES: Vault toilets; group
picnic shelter; hitch-
ing rails, feed
troughs, and spring
for horses; rentable
guard station; no
piped water for
humans; no garbage
service

PARKING: At individual site

FEE: No fee

ELEVATION: 6,050 feet

RESTRICTIONS: Pets: On leash
Fires: In fire pits
only
Alcohol: Permitted
Vehicles: Not recom-
mended for RVs or
trailers

experience to let a few 250-pound cougars ruin it. However, it's worth checking with the ranger station before
you go to see if there have been any incidents. Maybe
that nice-looking couple in their ready-for-action tennis
shoes have the right idea after all . . .

The campground at Godman is a terribly uncom-
plicated affair and very nearly unrecognizable as a
campground unless you get out of the car and walk
around. There are eight sites—so they say—and if this
place is ever full, I'm Sacajawea's illegitimate great-
great-great-granddaughter! The most obvious sites are
wrapped around the side of the heavily wooded ridge
where FS 46 turns west into deep, dark unknowns and
leaves the campground in a matter of seconds. There
are a couple of sites tucked back along a brushy spur
road of sorts, but that looked like cougar-snoozing territory to me, so I wimped out on investigating further.
You go first.

In the clearing below the road, the Godman
Guard Station is a surprising discovery even though I
knew about it before I visited the campground. Built in
the feverish 1930s by the Civilian Conservation Corps
(those guys were everywhere!), the cabin is not doing
much guarding these days but is fully furnished and
available for rent year-round (although winter requires
one have the fortitude of the Nez Perce, whose numbers were once great, to get in here via skis, snow-
shoes, or snowmobile). Even more surprising, the
cabin didn't appear to be rented at the height of the
summer season, so it seems reasonable to imagine
snagging it when you want.

Fortunately, whoever found this elbow in the road
and claimed it for the Umatilla National Forest made
sure that the main attractions—views to the south and
west—were visible from every campsite. From this high
ridge literally at the western door of the Wenaha–
Tucannon Wilderness, gorgeous sunsets are the evening
entertainment while you're cooking dinner.

Daytime entertainment is also right at your fingertips. The 200-mile network of trails in the Wenaha–
Tucannon can be accessed from West Butte Creek Trail
3138. You could conceivably wander for days and
not see another living (two-footed) soul. You'll wear

MAP

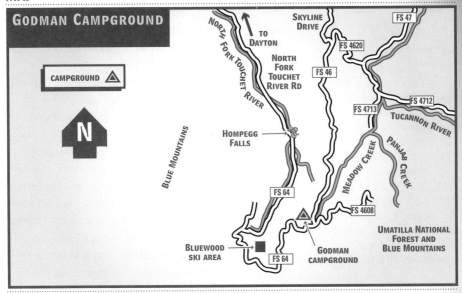

GODMAN CAMPGROUND

CAMPGROUND ▲

N

NORTH FORK TOUCHET RIVER

TO DAYTON

SKYLINE DRIVE

FS 47

FS 4620

NORTH FORK TOUCHET RIVER RD

FS 46

FS 4712

FS 4713

TUCANNON RIVER

HOMPEGG FALLS

BLUE MOUNTAINS

MEADOW CREEK

PANJAB CREEK

FS 64

FS 4608

UMATILLA NATIONAL FOREST AND BLUE MOUNTAINS

BLUEWOOD SKI AREA

FS 64

GODMAN CAMPGROUND

---

yourself out in the process. Most of the trails in the Wenaha–Tucannon make steep, abrupt drops into the river and creek canyons only to climb back up through thick forests of fir, spruce, pine, hemlock, and western larch to the expansive plateaus. It's a roller-coaster ride through the Wenaha–Tucannon.

If you want to start high and stay high, the best route is the ridgetop run 3113—known as Mount Misery Trail—that connects Teepee Trailhead (just below Godman at 5,400 feet) and Diamond Trail, which leaves from the base of Diamond Peak, the second-highest point in the wilderness at 6,379 feet. The trail skirts Oregon Butte, the wilderness's high point at 6,401 feet with a side trip to a lookout with jaw-dropping, 360-degree views!

GETTING THERE

From Dayton, turn right on CR 118, which starts as Eckler Mountain Road and becomes Skyline Drive. Drive 14 miles to FS 46 (a continuation of Skyline Drive) and follow it 11 miles to the campground. Have very good county and Forest Service maps with you both to find Godman and to more deeply explore the labyrinth of roads in lower Columbia County.

PALOUSE FALLS STATE PARK CAMPGROUND

> *A spectacular falls in the middle of the eastern Washington steppes and a fantastic spot for camping . . . if you can manage to have it to yourself.*

I **HAPPENED TO PICK UP** a copy of Ron Judd's *Camping! Washington* (Sasquatch Books) not long after I got back from a research trip to southeastern Washington and was thumbing through that section of his book. I laughed out loud when I read his entry for Palouse Falls State Park.

Sorry, Ron. Guilty as charged! On a stinking hot summer morning (in Bellingham), I packed up the car, picked up a friend, and made a beeline for the remote reaches of Washington's famous grasslands. And I have to say that, despite the minimal offerings at Palouse Falls, there are certain redeeming tent camping qualities about the park that make it imperative for me to fly directly in the face of your highly reasonable advice and recommend it to my readers.

First, no one in their right mind would imagine camping there, so you'll have the place to yourself by sundown (at least the camping area), right?

Second, this is a world away from anything that westsiders experience on a daily basis and just from sheer novelty gets my vote.

Third, the place is too full of geological and archaeological significance to imagine that the parks department would close this facility. And the more people that use it, the less chance of a closure. They've already been forced to do that with Lyons Ferry, Central Ferry, and Chief Timothy State Parks. A disturbing trend, to be sure.

Fourth, in light of point three, there aren't nearly the camping options in this region that there were even as recently as a year ago, so from a tent-camping standpoint, Palouse Falls is a winner. Perhaps the long-term plan, given the closure of the much larger neighboring facilities, is to make improvements to Palouse Falls. One can only hope.

On that note, I should prepare you in advance for

RATINGS

Beauty: ☆ ☆ ☆ ☆ ☆
Privacy: ☆
Spaciousness: ☆ ☆ ☆ ☆ ☆
Quiet: ☆ ☆ ☆ ☆ ☆
Security: ☆ ☆
Cleanliness: ☆ ☆ ☆ ☆ ☆

what you'll find: very little in the way of campground amenities. But much in the way of atmosphere, adventure, and austerity.

The camping area is nothing more than an open, grassy patch with a few spindly shade trees up to the left as you drive in. Yup, that's it. There are raised brazier grills positioned in an attempt to define individual sites, but for the most part, spacing will be determined by how much each camping party is willing to concede. If you're inclined toward sprawl, the spaces are going to get small in a hurry.

Let's put it in perspective. The entire park sits on 105 acres, and that includes a fair bit of land that is mostly undeveloped and through which trails wind along the canyon rim to various overlooks for viewing the falls. The camping area is part of only two acres that includes the picnicking area as well. The parking lot is bigger than the campground, if that helps give you a visual. Whatever you do, don't rely on the State Park Web site to give you a picture of camping at Palouse Falls. It's not so much what they say about the place, it's what they don't say. Based on their information, you would be tempted to come here expecting to find more of, well . . . a campground.

I hope you realize that this information is not meant to deter you. I just think it's important for you to know the score so there are no recriminations later. If the utmost in simplified camping is your style, then Palouse Falls will tickle you to no end.

Since the main attraction isn't the campground anyway, let's focus on what is: Palouse Falls, best visited in spring and early summer when the Palouse River dumps tons of water carrying tons of rich Palouse topsoil over the edge. It's a staggering scene but not exactly a pretty picture, with volumes of water about the color of a Starbuck's double tall mocha with plenty of extra foam roaring into a 200-foot chasm. Later in the season, the flow becomes much clearer and also much quieter, enhancing the scale of the tortured basalt walls that form the deep amphitheater. There's a Native American legend about those walls. Interpretive signs around the canyon perimeter tell of the creation of Palouse Falls and its singular impor-

KEY INFORMATION

ADDRESS:	Palouse Falls State Park P.O. Box 157 Starbuck, WA 99359
OPERATED BY:	Washington State Parks and Recreation Commission
INFORMATION:	(360) 902-8844 (Washington State Parks information center)
OPEN:	All year
SITES:	10 tent-only sites
EACH SITE HAS:	Picnic table; raised brazier
ASSIGNMENT:	First come, first served
REGISTRATION:	On site
FACILITIES:	Restrooms; picnic area; dump station; no garbage service
PARKING:	In general parking area
FEE:	$10
ELEVATION:	750 feet
RESTRICTIONS:	**Pets:** On leash **Fires:** No wood fires allowed **Alcohol:** Permitted **Vehicles:** No RV or pickup-camper parking

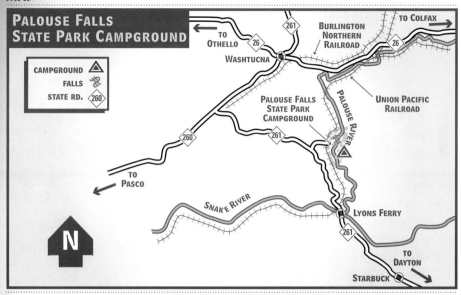

GETTING THERE

From Washtucna at the intersection of WA 260/261, go about 6 miles south to the junction of 260 and 261. Turn left (southwest) onto WA 261 and drive 14.5 miles to Palouse Falls Road. Turn left and follow it to its end at the park (less than 2 miles).

tance as the vestige of a dramatic geologic event 15,000 years ago. If you want to read an excellent technical account of the shaping of this natural wonder, get a copy of *Hiking Washington's Geology* (The Mountaineers). A good book to keep in the glove compartment (right beside this guide).

Just as fascinating as the falls is the Marmes Rock Shelter, where human remains have been dated as some of the oldest found in the Western Hemisphere (roughly 10,000 years). You can access this site from the (former) Lyons Ferry State Park parking lot, assuming it is still accessible despite the park's closure.

TUCANNON CAMPGROUND

IN A DAUNTING no-man's-land of steep-walled river canyons, smooth-topped tablelands, and harsh climatic extremes where the greatest populations are hooved, furry, and winged inhabitants, the Umatilla National Forest straddles some of the loneliest country in Washington and Oregon.

This is great territory in which to simply lose yourself in the elements. Whether that means a contented afternoon fly-fishing on Big Four Pond, a brisk morning mountain bike whirl up dusty canyon roads, birdwatching on Skyline Drive, or a contemplative ramble on the Tucannon River Trail, the activity is only an excuse to immerse yourself in the unique environs of the Umatilla National Forest.

For any of these pursuits, Tucannon Campground is a base camp extraordinaire that sits alongside its namesake river in the northern reach of the Umatilla Forest. It is no exaggeration to say that Tucannon Campground can easily be considered the last "civilized" outpost for anyone venturing into the belly of the Blue Mountains and the Wenaha–Tucannon Wilderness of southeastern Washington. Deep in that belly, Tucannon River starts as a tiny freshet high on the slope of Diamond Peak and takes a convoluted journey northwestward through a series of canyons, hollows, valleys, gulches, and flats before giving itself up to the Snake River at the southern border of the Palouse.

Frankly, it's surprising to find any kind of developed campground out here other than for hunters trying to outnumber their prey, the largest Rocky Mountain elk herd in the country. Elk hunting has been the #1 recreation activity for many years on the Umatilla, but the popularity of fishing—as evidenced by the plethora of fishing holes and camping options dispersed all along Tucannon Road—and the desire for

> *The lonely country of the Umatilla National Forest is the backdrop for the "civilized" outpost at Tucannon.*

RATINGS

Beauty: ✿ ✿ ✿ ✿ ✿
Privacy: ✿ ✿ ✿ ✿ ✿
Spaciousness: ✿ ✿ ✿ ✿ ✿
Quiet: ✿ ✿ ✿ ✿ ✿
Security: ✿ ✿ ✿
Cleanliness: ✿ ✿ ✿ ✿ ✿

KEY INFORMATION

ADDRESS: Tucannon Campground
c/o Pomeroy Ranger District
71 West Main
Pomeroy, WA 99347

OPERATED BY: Umatilla National Forest

INFORMATION: (509) 843-1891

OPEN: Early spring–late fall

SITES: 15

EACH SITE HAS: Picnic table; fire pit with grill

ASSIGNMENT: First come, first served

REGISTRATION: On site

FACILITIES: Vault toilets; no piped water; no garbage service

PARKING: At individual site

FEE: $5

ELEVATION: 2,600 feet

RESTRICTIONS: Pets: On leash
Fires: In fire pits only
Alcohol: Permitted
Vehicles: Trailers and RVs up to 15 feet long

more remote backpacking options is starting to bring in new user groups.

What's even more amazing is discovering that Tucannon shares its riverside real estate with Camp Wooten Environmental Learning Center. This group facility that can handle as many as 200 people has a rustic splendor reminiscent of the 1930s (when the Civilian Conservation Corps built it) and even sports an indoor swimming pool! Welcome to the wilderness!

In keeping with the (mostly) rustic ambience of Camp Wooten, Tucannon Campground is an amicable collection of 14 tent sites that range from open and grassy spots on the Tucannon River side to cloistered and brushy spots that back up to little Hixon Creek as it cuts through the southeastern corner of the camp. All feature plenty of elbow room, however. If you're the kind of camper that brings lots of creature comforts to support your civilized lifestyle, know that Tucannon sites are made to handle your load—probably with room to spare. Bring the Mongolian tent. There's room for the whole tribe!

Another nice feature at Tucannon is that every campsite is close to its parking area. I love these old campgrounds that understand the dignity of maintaining a greenbelt between campsite and car. Foliage throughout Tucannon is plentiful and impressive, with stately ponderosas presiding over the scene.

Perhaps Tucannon's best feature is apparent even before you get there—the winding, scenic drive along the Tucannon Road—paved the entire way! History and geology are juxtaposed as roadside markers point out the return route of Lewis and Clark as they followed the contours of the land over bunchgrass flats rising and falling between jutting basalt outcroppings and sharp ridges. Looking at the landscape today—unchanged except for a few more structures sprinkled across the open terrain—one can identify with the explorers' wonderment at this grand and strange land. Such an open book on one hand, full of mysteries still to be revealed on the other.

It's actually an upside-down world, which is one of the reasons it perplexes newcomers. Where most mountainous landscapes are a study in river valleys that

MAP

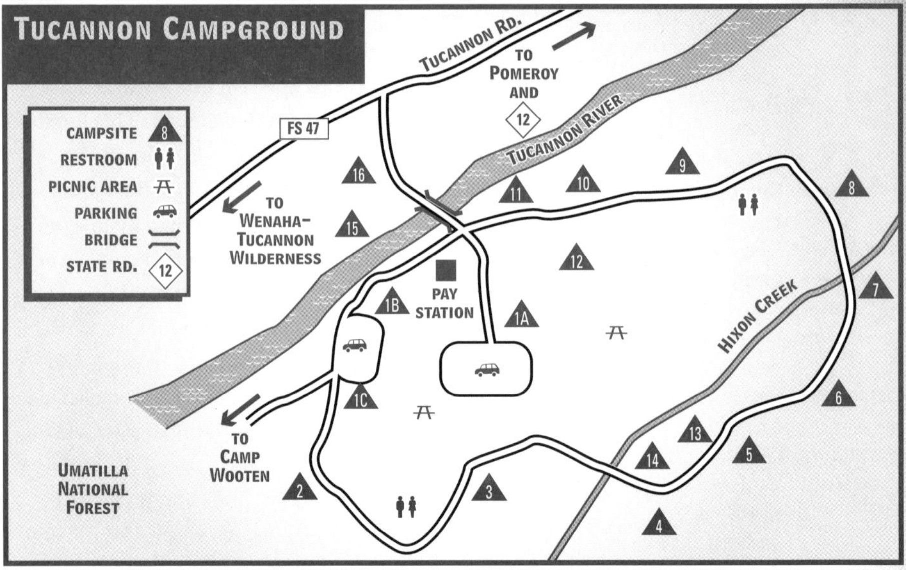
TUCANNON CAMPGROUND
CAMPSITE
RESTROOM
PICNIC AREA
PARKING
BRIDGE
STATE RD.
12
TUCANNON RD.
TO POMEROY AND
12
FS 47
TUCANNON RIVER
TO WENAHA-TUCANNON WILDERNESS
PAY STATION
HIXON CREEK
TO CAMP WOOTEN
UMATILLA NATIONAL FOREST
1A
1B
1C
2
3
4
5
6
7
8
9
10
11
12
13
14
15
16

have been gouged and carved by advancing glaciers, the Umatilla was born of upsurging basalt that laid a thick volcanic blanket. Over time, rivers wore through the rock and created the deep canyons we peer down into today. Aerial views of the region are the best way to see how this geologic story unfolded. Short of that, a driving tour along the plateau rims makes a good substitute and a great excuse for a picnic.

Keep in mind as you are exploring the Umatilla and its wilderness areas that this is a place where wildlife abounds and generally outnumbers people. The forest supports habitat for black bear, deer, bighorn sheep, Rocky Mountain elk, cougar, bobcat, coyote, and pine martens. The bird population is equal parts migratory and resident, and more than 200 species have been identified on the Umatilla.

Field guides are handy companions out here, as is a full tank of gas.

GETTING THERE

From Pomeroy on WA 12, turn south on CR 101 and travel 17 miles, then go 4 miles south on FS 47. Take FS 160 to the left, and the campground is a few hundred yards across the Tucannon River.

APPENDIXES

APPENDIX A
CAMPING EQUIPMENT
CHECKLIST

Except for the large and bulky items on this list, I keep a plastic storage container full of the essentials for car camping so they're ready to go when I am. I make a last-minute check of the inventory, resupply anything that's low or missing, and away I go!

COOKING UTENSILS
Bottle opener
Bottles of salt, pepper, spices, sugar, cooking oil, and maple syrup in waterproof, spill-proof containers
Can opener
Corkscrew
Cups, plastic or tin
Dish soap (biodegradable), sponge, and towel
Drinking water container (nonbreakable)
Flatware
Food of your choice
Frying pan
Fuel for stove
Matches in waterproof container
Plates
Pocketknife
Pot with lid
Potholder
Spatula
Stove
Tin foil
Wooden spoon

FIRST AID KIT
Band-Aids
First-aid cream
Gauze pads
Ibuprofen or aspirin
Insect repellent
Moleskin
Snakebite kit (if you're heading for desert conditions)
Sunscreen/Chapstick

Tape, waterproof adhesive

SLEEPING GEAR
Pillow
Sleeping bag
Sleeping pad, inflatable or insulated
Tent with ground tarp and rainfly

MISCELLANEOUS
Bath soap (biodegradable), washcloth, and towel
Camp chair
Candles
Cooler
Deck of cards
Fire starter
Flashlight with fresh batteries
Foul weather clothing (useful year-round in the Northwest)
Paper towels
Plastic zip-top bags
Sunglasses
Toilet paper
Water bottle
Wool blanket

OPTIONAL
Barbecue grill
Binoculars
Books on bird, plant, and wildlife identification
Fishing rod and tackle
Hatchet
Lantern
Maps (road, topographic, trails, etc.)

APPENDIX B
SOURCES OF
INFORMATION

AAA AUTOMOBILE CLUB OF WASHINGTON
330 Sixth Avenue North
Seattle, WA 98109
(206) 448-5353
www.aaa.com

CASCADE BICYCLE CLUB
7400 Sand Point Way NE
P.O. Box 15165
Seattle, WA 98115
(206) 522-3222 or
(206) 522-BIKE (ride-description hotline)
www.cascade.org

**LAKE ROOSEVELT NATIONAL RECREATION
AREA** *(National Park Service)*
1008 Crest Drive
Coulee Dam, WA 99116
(509) 633-9441
www.nps.gov/laro

MOUNT RAINIER NATIONAL PARK
(National Park Service)
Tahoma Woods, Star Route
Ashford, WA 98304
(360) 569-2211
www.nps.gov/mora

**MOUNT ST. HELENS NATIONAL VOLCANIC
MONUMENT** *(U.S. Forest Service)*
42218 NE Yale Bridge Road
Amboy, WA 98601
(360) 247-3900 or (360) 247-3903 (visitor
center; 24-hour information)
www.fs.fed.us/gpnf/mshnvm

THE MOUNTAINEERS
(hiking and climbing club)
300 Third Avenue West
Seattle, WA 98119
(206) 284-6310
www.mountaineers.org

**NATIONAL RECREATION RESERVATION
SYSTEM (NRRS)**
(877) 444-6777
www.reserveUSA.com

NATURE OF THE NORTHWEST
(maps and field guides)
800 NE Oregon, #5
Portland, OR 97232
(503) 731-4444
www.naturenw.org

NORTH CASCADES NATIONAL PARK
(National Park Service)
2105 WA 20
Sedro Woolley, WA 98284
(360) 856-5700
www.nps.gov/noca

**NORTHWEST INTERPRETIVE
ASSOCIATION**
(nonprofit information service)
909 First Avenue, Suite 630
Seattle, WA 98104
(206) 220-4140
www.nwpubliclands.com

APPENDIX B
SOURCES OF
INFORMATION

(continued)

OLYMPIC NATIONAL PARK
(National Park Service)
600 East Park Avenue
Port Angeles, WA 98362
(360) 452-4501
www.nps.gov/olym

OUTDOOR RECREATION INFORMATION
(National Park Service and U.S. Forest Service information for Washington, Oregon, and Idaho)
222 Yale North (inside REI)
Seattle, WA 98109-5429
(206) 220-7450

U.S. FOREST SERVICE
(Pacific Northwest Regional Headquarters)
P.O. Box 3623, Portland, OR 97208
333 SW First Avenue, Portland, OR 97204
(503) 221-2877
www.fs.fed.us/r6

WASHINGTON KAYAK CLUB
P.O. Box 24264
Seattle, WA 98124
(206) 433-1983
www.washingtonkayakclub.org

WASHINGTON STATE DEPARTMENT OF COMMERCE AND ECONOMIC DEVELOPMENT, TOURISM DIVISION
P.O. Box 42500
Olympia, WA 98504-2500
(800) 544-1800
www.tourism.wa.gov

WASHINGTON STATE DEPARTMENT OF NATURAL RESOURCES
P.O. Box 47001
Olympia, WA 98504-7001
(360) 902-1000 or (800) 527-3305
www.wadnr.gov

WASHINGTON STATE DEPARTMENT OF FISH AND WILDLIFE
600 Capitol Way North
Olympia, WA 98501
(360) 902-2200
http://wdfw.wa.gov

WASHINGTON STATE PARKS AND RECREATION COMMISSION
P.O. Box 42650
Olympia, WA 98504-2650
(800) 233-0321
www.parks.wa.gov

WASHINGTON TRAILS ASSOCIATION
1305 Fourth Avenue, Suite 512
Seattle, WA 98101
(206) 625-1367
www.wta.org

WASHINGTON WATER TRAILS ASSOCIATION
4649 Sunnyside Avenue North, #305
Seattle, WA 98103
(206) 545-9161
www.wwta.org

INDEX

ABOUT THE AUTHOR

JEANNE LOUISE PYLE is a transplanted Marylander who has lived in the Pacific Northwest for 30 years. Her love of the outdoors led to authoring the first book of *The Best in Tent Camping* series in 1994. Pyle currently resides in Bellingham, Washington.